Whenever I have participated with the author in conferences and classes there has been à rich deposit of God's presence and grace on both men and women, leaders and workers. This book takes this dynamic to another level of impact to the church in the partnership of men and women in effective ministry.

—JOSEPH UMIDI, D.MIN.
PROFESSOR, REGENT UNIVERSITY
PASTOR, NEW LIFE CHRISTIAN FELLOWSHIP
VIRGINIA BEACH, VIRGINIA

Joyce Strong joins the symphony of prophetic voices from history and from the new millennium, forming a chorus of gospel proclamation: Christ as Reconciler has reconciled male and female in Him to become one in relationship, ministry and mission. Joyce Strong's practical, yet moving apologetic supporting women's full participation as coheirs of the kingdom is written from the heart of one whose words clearly echo the voice of the Father's heart.

—THE REVEREND MARA LIEF CRABTREE, D.MIN.
ASSOCIATE PROFESSOR OF CHRISTIAN SPIRITUALITY
AND WOMEN'S STUDIES
REGENT UNIVERSITY SCHOOL OF DIVINITY
VIRGINIA BEACH, VIRGINIA

It's you! It's me! It's many women we know! For me personally, this book has 'opened the windows of heaven.' It has propelled me out of mediocrity and given me the push to "press in" and "press on" in unabashed obedience to what God wants to do in and through me. Fear has broken off and fallen away.

—DEBI MOTT
DIRECTOR OF WOMEN'S MINISTRIES
KEMPSVILLE PRESBYTERIAN CHURCH
VIRGINIA BEACH, VIRGINIA

INSTRUMENTS
for
H I S
Glory

INSTRUMENTS
for
H I S
Glory

JOYCE STRONG

CREATION
HOUSE

INSTRUMENTS FOR HIS GLORY by Joyce Strong
Published by Creation House
Strang Communications Company
600 Rinehart Road
Lake Mary, Florida 32746
www.creationhouse.com
www.charismalife.com

Unless otherwise noted, Scripture quotations are from the Holy
Bible, New International Version. Copyright © 1973, 1978, 1984,
International Bible Society. Used by permission.

Incidents and persons portrayed in this volume are based on fact.
However, some names and details have been changed to protect
the privacy of the individuals.

Library of Congress Cataloging-in-Publication Data

Strong, Joyce.
  Instruments for His glory / Joyce Strong.
     p. cm
  ISBN 0-88419-646-1
  Includes bibliographical references.
  I. Women clergy. I. Title.
BV676.S77 1999
282'.14'082—dc21   99-27659
                                                          CIP

9 0 1 2 3 4 5 BBG 8 7 6 5 4 3 2 1
Printed in the United States of America

To those brave ladies who have gone before us, following the Call against great odds, showing us the grace of God.

And to the next generation to come, may you play for the Maestro with courage and humility, truly instruments for His glory.

Acknowledgments

Special love and thanks to:

- *D. Kirkland,* for her visionary encouragement and practical help as this book came into its final form and for her longing to sit at Jesus' feet.

- *Donna Paulk,* for faithfully and tirelessly surrounding me with prayer for some two years now and for speaking prophetically into my life.

- *Pastor Marie Pogorelec,* for her sensitivity to the Holy Spirit and for showing me that gifted, godly women can truly be instruments for His glory from the pulpit.

- *Debi Mott,* for her loving exuberance and wisdom, her selfless service to others and her vision for women to mature in the church.

- *Diane Chandler,* for her hunger and obedience, her sensible devotion to a higher call and her gift of promoting others in the kingdom.

- *Darla Scheideman,* for her transparency and passion as a leader on her knees.

- *All the women in ministry* who thoughtfully and candidly responded to my questionnaire. Humbly press on. He will fulfill His plans for you!

- *Brenda Davis,* editor of *SpiritLed Woman,* and *Joy Strang,* publisher, for breaking new ground in Christian publishing to help women everywhere become instruments for His glory.

Contents

✣

Foreword

God has a plan for you, and we want to help you fulfill it. *SpiritLed Woman* magazine and Creation House are excited to present SpiritLed Woman books to challenge you to grow spiritually and address practical life issues with spiritual insight.

The leaders of *SpiritLed Woman* magazine are pleased to introduce to you *Instruments for His Glory* by Joyce Strong. More and more areas of service and calling are opening for women, but many of those gifted and called by God often struggle because they lack guidance. *Instruments for His Glory* offers sensible, honest biblical counsel with encouragement and instruction from one who has been there for twenty-two years and is now a popular speaker at women's conferences, retreats and seminars.

Joyce Strong understands her audience. Using wonderful illustrations from the lives of historical and contemporary women, she lovingly and firmly uncovers and addresses the deep issues that women face as they seek to obey the calling of God upon their lives. *Instruments for His Glory* provides a very balanced application of spiritual truth for a woman's journey into service for the Lord Jesus Christ.

The leaders of *SpiritLed Woman* magazine believe that *Instruments for His Glory* will greatly enrich you as you seek to serve the Lord and will help empower you to walk the Spirit-led life.

—BRENDA DAVIS, EDITOR
SPIRITLED WOMAN MAGAZINE

Preface

As I peered out my classroom window at Teen Challenge through the foggy drizzle that had wrapped the wooded hillside in gloom all day, a dream took root in my heart: Someday I would write a book to encourage women called to minister in the body of Christ.

That was nearly fifteen years ago, and now the time has come. Back then I could hear only my own voice crying for help. Today, God has taken me into a wider arena, and I hear hundreds of women's voices filling the air, like the sound of a river cascading from rocky places into a deep canyon below.

I see their faces everywhere—in the seminaries, church pews, Bible schools and women's conferences at which I speak—and it is as though I were looking into a mirror at my own reflection. They—and I—dare to believe that what we have heard God whisper to our spirits will come to pass.

Our visions camp within our briefcases, and our dreams invade our grocery lists. In the stillness of the night, God's Spirit calls to ours—before the expectations of others call to us at sunrise. To whose voice should we respond? In which direction should we go?

God has given us the visions, dreams and call, but those around us are not so quick to understand—nor are we at times! Furthermore, our self-doubts and our hunger for approval often stymie our obedience.

God is calling us to get serious—to ask Him to search our hearts for weaknesses, allowing Him to deal with them. He calls us to prepare ourselves diligently and humbly and to yield to His wisdom for our timing in everything. If we are ill-prepared, hasty or irresponsible, we will alienate those whom we love and seek to serve, and we will humiliate ourselves—thus taking one step *forward* and three steps *backward*.

But move we must, for God has truly called us to serve Him in a more public way. For too long we have remained on the sidelines, letting culture dictate silence and inactivity.

It is imperative that we see ourselves as our Father sees

us—not as man sees us—and to obey Him at every turn. He will never ask us to violate His own laws of love nor all that is feminine within us. We have nothing to fear.

GOD'S DREAM

God has given me a vivid picture of the way in which He wants women to minister alongside men in the body of Christ. Together we are to be a royal Symphony, expressing order and unity, mutual respect and diversity, obedience to the Holy Spirit's score and unlimited love for the Maestro.

This beloved Maestro will be neither man nor woman, but God Himself! Under His leadership we will play in harmony by the power of the Holy Spirit, with Christ as our example. Someday *His* music will flow through us, free of the fear of man. Someday all the power struggles, pride, insecurity and wounds will be yielded, and we will serve Him together in confidence and humility.

Someday men and women will minister side by side without thought to gender, sensitive to God's anointing alone. *Together* we will reveal the unbroken image of God to those who have never known Him, and together we will celebrate His goodness.

But first He will make us into instruments for His glory. We must learn quickly to create the music with the power of His grace—for the promise is drawing near!

Part One

Passion: The Melody Deep Within

The children were finally asleep. The radiators crackled, pouring warmth throughout the drafty rooms of the rambling farmhouse tucked away in the Western Pennsylvania mountains. The heat subdued the cold, persistently pressing it down to the worn floors and into the far corners of each room.

Janet snuggled up next to her sleeping husband, Enoch. Rubbing her cold feet together within the warm folds of her flannel nightgown, she was careful not to let them touch Enoch. She didn't want to wake him; it was Saturday night, and Enoch must preach in the morning.

The moon sent a cool, white wave of light through the flowered curtains, causing shadows of undulating, bare tree branches to scurry back and forth across the bedroom wall in a gentle rhythm. Janet hoped the rhythm would lull her to sleep.

Her mind was filled again, just as it had been for as long as she could remember. The faces of her neighbors paraded before her eyes. Teens like Mark and Cody, who passed notes to the girls during every church service...Mr. Cratser and his unhappy-looking new wife...Donna Minor and the three small children she was raising alone...There were others she didn't recognize, who seemed to be waiting for her to say something that would make a difference in their lives. Their struggles, joys, confusions and heartaches were an inescapable part of her life—and she longed somehow to shepherd them.

Since she had been a little girl she had dreamed of preaching. Sermons sprang to life within her heart and mind at almost any time of day or night.

But she was a woman, and the year was 1955. Women simply were not pastors—particularly not in her conservative church! Women were meant to teach children and one another, sort clothing for the missionaries and periodically prepare fellowship meals for the congregation. They certainly did not preach! Janet's dream of preaching must remain just that—a dream.

The sleeping man beside her would be the preacher tomorrow. Still, the passion in her heart burned on in silence.

1

An Irresistible Song

For God did not give us a spirit of timidity, but a spirit of power, of love and of self-discipline.
—2 TIMOTHY 1:7

The intensity of the cry from deep within our hearts to minister comes in direct response to what God has done for us. As we experience forgiveness, we long to tell others of the blessed freedom of transformation; as we learn to obey the great principles of God's Word, we long to bear wonderful fruit that we can give to others. We feel a distinct tugging within toward one specific form of ministry, and our hearts jump at the thought of fulfilling that call.

The Lord's indescribable love for us enlarges our human passion for destiny and significance far beyond its natural boundaries, transforming it into a deep spiritual burden for others.

His heart has begun to beat within our own.

OUR SPIRITUAL HERITAGE

If we study the lives of great women of faith from past centuries—the most "unliberated" of times—we will be deeply moved and encouraged. In the seventeenth century, Jeanne Guyon shook the throne of France and influenced some of the most respected names in church history with her writings on the believer's need for intimacy with Christ. The fact that she ended up in the Bastille for writing *The Song of the Bride* mattered little to her. Her books are still changing lives nearly four hundred years later.

In more recent times, when Victorian restraints were great against women's public and spiritual leadership in the United States and England—the late nineteenth and early twentieth centuries—several women turned the system upside down.

Catherine Booth, the cofounder of the Salvation Army, preached to millions of men and women before her death in 1890. She raised four daughters, all of whom became evangelists. Her oldest daughter first spoke in public at age thirteen and went on to become a far-reaching evangelist while raising eight children of her own.[1]

Jesse Penn-Lewis, an Englishwoman whom God used powerfully to preach the gospel around the same time as Booth, was described by Dr. R. A. Torrey as "one of the most gifted speakers the world has known."[2] Some of the struggles and prejudice she faced are seen in these comments recorded by her biographer:

> I saw that God had given me a specific commission to proclaim the message of the cross at a time when it had almost ceased to be referred to in the pulpits. I saw also that God miraculously opened doors before me to proclaim this message, which no man could shut, but that the one objection was the fact that I was a woman. There was no quarrel with the message, there was no denial of the divine seal, there was no getting away from the evidence of the results. But none of these things did away with the fact that I was a woman, and therefore I could not but see that whilst God opened doors for me in some quarters, others were fast closed to the message I bore, purely and only because I was a woman....
>
> I knew only too well what the letter of the Scripture said in just three passages of the apostle Paul's writings, but I was certain in my mind as I walked with God and found His will and guidance, and as His message came to me, that if we only knew the exact original meaning of those passages, they were bound to be in harmony with the working of the Holy Spirit in the nineteenth

century. I no longer say to the Lord, "Why hast Thou made me a woman?" My spirit is now at rest, and I see why, in spite of all my endeavors by prayer and action to retire from the commission which was directly laid upon me, I was not able to get free, for God had a deeper intention in making me a woman and giving me the marked approval and guidance of His Spirit in the service He had called me to.[3]

To Henrietta Mears, who taught and inspired such outstanding leaders as Bill Bright, the founder of Campus Crusade for Christ, and Richard Halverson, chaplain of the United States Senate, Dr. Harold John Ockenga once wrote:

When I think of the tens of thousands of people who have studied the Bible under your leadership ... of the hundreds of young men who have gone into the ministry, and other young people into Christian service, I cannot but stand back in amazement.[4]

And the list goes on to include Emma Dryer, who worked with D. L. Moody to found the Moody Bible Institute; Dorothy Ruth Miller, a great Bible teacher who was once offered the chair of Bible at Wheaton College; and Amy Lee Stockton, a tremendously qualified preacher who was endorsed by the outstanding theologian Dr. G. Campbell Morgan.

FAR-REACHING SIGNIFICANCE

Church history is rich with amazing stories of the significant contributions of women preachers. In fact, every revival has been accompanied by the renewed ministry of consecrated women who preached the gospel!

Therefore, it is not surprising that women, especially in America, have been in the forefront of supporting and funding overseas missions. One hundred twenty-five years ago women outnumbered men two to one! (Today, the ratio is six women to four men.) "The more difficult and dangerous the work, the higher the ratio of women to men."[5] Unlike service in the organized church, access to the mission field was based more upon *gifting* and *passion* than on *gender* and *ordination*.

Furthermore, these women were amazing! Amy Carmichael, who founded the Dohnavur Fellowship of India, served by faith in the manner of George Müller, who made his needs known to God alone and saw His miraculous provision. Malla Moe was one of the longest-serving and most fruitful missionaries to South Africa. Louisa Vaughan and Gladys Aylward were pioneers in China.

These—and many other—women preachers and missionaries persisted and triumphed because of their commitment, courage, self-sacrifice and the blessing of God. By answering the call of God with a pure heart and deep conviction, they were able to perform mighty deeds in difficult times. Regardless of the cultural mind-set of the church, women of obedience and unwavering faith took their places to break down the gates of hell and set the captives free.

SUBMITTED WOMEN OF CONVICTION

These ladies were not renegades. They moved cautiously by the Holy Spirit but with the deep conviction that God had indeed called them to preach and teach the gospel to men and women alike. And in each case, there were brave men in spiritual authority who recognized the anointing of God on these mighty women's lives, who championed their cause and who encouraged them.

KEYS TO SPIRITUAL SUCCESS

What enabled these women to follow the irresistible song of the Savior into culturally alien territory? What keys could they pass on to us to unlock spiritual effectiveness in our own lives? As I studied their lives and ministries, these keys stood out. Each of these women possessed:

- *Intimacy with God,* which enabled them to hear from Him.
- *Consuming love* for the lost.
- *Self-sacrifice* and surrender of earthly rewards.
- *Diligence* even when only God was watching.
- *Faithfulness* to those who depended upon them.
- *Forgiveness* when misunderstood.

- *Respect* for authority.
- *Undivided hearts* fixed on righteousness.
- *Willingness* to wait, to suffer and to learn.
- *Utter obedience to God* and devotion to His Word.

GREATNESS

The greatness of any ministry we give, as well as the very strength of our lives, will depend upon how seriously we take our God and how willing we are to be obedient to Him. When we have walked the way of the cross and have died to selfish ambition, and when we see ourselves as responsible parts of the body of Christ, God will make a way where there seems to be no way!

He will provide champions of our cause from among godly men—men who understand that headship means to be a "source of life" to the women God gives them to serve and lead. By these men—and by other godly women around us—we will be encouraged, equipped and given valuable accountability as we serve in harmony with others in the body.

GOD IS COMMITTED TO US

Of this we can be sure: God is completely committed to us! He is in this relationship with us for the long haul, and He wills us to be victorious in Him! His strength will be made perfect in our weakness (2 Cor. 12:9).

Even if the future looks uncertain to us now—obstacles

seemingly insurmountable and the passion strong but unful-filled—we need not be discouraged. As we step forward in obedience to His Spirit within and say, "Here I am, Lord; use me," He will bring to pass what He has called us to do.

But first He will make us women of authentic virtue. Personal integrity, peace in adversity, obedience of heart and the willingness to wait are lessons that precede any action of lasting value. He is not in a hurry, and He does not want us to be discordant distractions, doing more harm than good. It is His plan to make us instruments for His glory, fit to play in the Symphony to come!

Going Deeper

1. Besides a deep concern for the lost, why do you think many women in the nineteenth century became involved in funding, directing and participating in overseas missions?

2. What do you suppose happened to female leadership of missions when the missions were denominationalized?

3. How could women exercise leadership as Christians in the United States during the late nineteenth and early twentieth centuries?

4. Who are your contemporary spiritual heroines in the ministry? Why do you admire them?

5. What are some of the obstacles women face when called to preach or pastor today in the United States?

6. Describe an opening to minister that God obviously provided for you when normally a woman would not have been allowed to minister. Did God also provide a male "champion" to help make it happen?

7. With which of the ten marks of greatness can you identify? With which of these is God dealing in your life now?

Prayer of Commitment for Today:

2

⁂

Striking a Chord

Just as each of us has one body with many members,
and these members do not all have the same function,
so in Christ we who are many form one body, and
each member belongs to all the others. We have dif-
ferent gifts, according to the grace given us.

—ROMANS 12:4–6

Effective ministry is a result of God-given passion, vision, gifting and timing. Any one of these qualities *alone*, without the others, will prove fruitless and perhaps even harmful. But together they release the anointing of the Holy Spirit to change lives.

Vision is a picture of what is not reality yet, but that which God has shown us can be. Passion is the fire that fuels vision, the energy that burns in our bones when we contemplate bringing that vision into reality. Without the divine encounter with God that creates passion, we will never have the strength to endure the rigors of the mission. And passion is rooted in love—the love relationship we have with God and the love He has given us to give to others. Passion without this love will be like a fire gone wild, never accomplishing anything but a selfish counterfeit of the real vision.

The timing for our release into the fulfillment of the vision will depend upon our maturity, while our specific roles will hinge upon the spiritual gifts with which God has equipped us.

SPIRITUAL GIFTS

It is exciting to discover the spiritual gifts God has put within us. We can start to identify them by asking some simple questions: What has always brought us unselfish delight? For what do people seek us out? What do people of spiritual discernment affirm in us? What can we "see" ourselves doing or being someday? About what kinds of ministries do we find ourselves praying most often? What is God quickening to us through His Word?

MY OWN JOURNEY OF DISCOVERY

As I look back over my own life, I can see that the first clue to my gifting was given to me by my second grade teacher. After watching me eagerly explain the mysteries of English or math to struggling classmates during recess, she wrote on my report card that I would surely become a teacher.

As I moved into junior and senior high school and my love for the Lord continued to grow, an ability to counsel became evident. It was not unusual for other students to pass me notes in study hall or to catch me on the bus to ask my advice about relationships in their lives. They seemed to know that I cared about them and would do my best to help them come to the right resolution.

As a young adult, whenever I saw others hurting or relating to one another negatively, God gave me the ability to *feel* what they were experiencing. I could often determine the root of their problems just by watching their reactions. I yearned to help them understand themselves and one another and find God's answer to their pain. The gifts of mercy and encouragement were developing in my spirit.

After our two children were in school, I was invited to teach at Teen Challenge Training Center. I began by teaching English, the area in which I had my college degree. But before long I implemented a remedial reading program in order to equip and encourage the men who were dropping out of the program simply because they couldn't read. I wanted deeply to see them succeed as believers in a difficult world.

Ultimately I developed courses on applying God's Word to problems in personal relationships. This was what made my heart sing with the greatest joy!

In the beginning of my work at Teen Challenge, I used my gifts of teaching and encouraging. When I developed the

Remedial Reading Department and trained student teachers to help me, God strengthened my gift of leadership, or administration as it is sometimes called.

Today, as I design seminars and retreats and speak on issues of integrity and spiritual maturity, God is adding to the mix the gift of prophecy so that I can be discerning as I respond to the needs in the body of Christ. While my passion to relieve pain—which has fueled my vision to see believers come to maturity—has changed little through the years, experience and training have released other gifts and given me many avenues through which I can minister.

The gifts that are least strong in us should not be ignored. It is important that we mature through the use of all the gifts. I have never tested high in the gifts of giving or serving, but I have been asking God to develop these within me as well. As I have stayed alert to the beauty of these gifts, God has given me special opportunities to serve behind the scenes in blessing others in physical and practical ways.

WE ARE NEEDED

Each of us is desperately needed to minister to the lost and to help bring the body of Christ to maturity. We must value and nurture the gifts that God has placed in us and act responsibly with them.

Above all we must remember that the point of God's gracing us with spiritual gifts is to build His kingdom—not to give us personal importance! The temptation to let the gifts define us becomes great if we lose focus or if we become the center of the service.

It is not about *us,* but about *Him.* We are simply His vessels.

GOD DIRECTS

God sometimes performs a "turnaround" in our lives in order to release spiritual gifts that we hadn't known were resident within.

Groomed for the stage and the opera since childhood, at twenty-two years of age Marilyn Burroughs was so close to singing in the Metropolitan Opera that she could taste it. While in her senior year at Houghton College in 1965 she was one of ten finalists.

One Sunday morning a young man who was preparing for the ministry invited her to go with him to a service at a small Salvation Army church in a neighboring town. It was during that service that God dramatically touched her life. The Holy Spirit arrested her afresh with the gospel and filled her with His presence, awakening within her a great love for the lost. This changed her destiny.

Within a year after both had finished school, she and Bill Francis—that young man who had taken her to the service— were married and headed for a ministry career with The Salvation Army. They are both colonels and ordained ministers and evangelists in the Army today.

As she looks back on that experience and the course her life has taken, she says, "God took me from the stage and put me on the street corner. Praise the Lord!" Marilyn now sings—and preaches—to reach the world for Christ.

WITHIN DENOMINATIONAL RESTRAINTS

While my own mother has a natural gift of teaching, I suspect that she has always been an evangelist at heart. But since women are not allowed to be evangelists or preachers in her denomination, God has given her other ways to reach the lost.

During the time that I was in grade school, she sold Bibles door to door to supplement what the family farm brought in. However, it was not a sale that brought her the greatest joy and about which she talked excitedly even years later. It was about how she had led a precious neighbor to the Lord, using the very Bible being considered for purchase! Her mountaintop experiences during those years occurred when she was able to pray with someone to accept Jesus into his or her life.

Later, when she taught in public schools, her motivation again was to reach some child with the saving grace of God. Now in her seventies, she teaches a Bible study in her home, always hoping the unsaved will attend so that she can have the privilege of leading them to the Lord.

She doesn't "work" at this. The passion is just there, and it burns deep. I believe God gave her the love of teaching so that she could have an avenue to reveal His heart to the lost without her having to be in a pulpit.

A TASTE OF "SYMPHONY"

Besides serving, teaching has been the most acceptable area of ministry for us in the body of Christ. However, it is becoming less uncommon for women with the gift of teaching to share the platform with men at conferences and seminars. How delightful to see the depth that prevails when men and women lead *together*, teach *together* and minister *together!* What a balance of wisdom and insight the two complements can give! We need one another in ministry; the fullest representation of God's heart and mind prevails when we serve as one.

An avenue that has opened to allow women into an administrative leadership position is that of becoming a church business administrator. Qualified women are being promoted from secretary or bookkeeper to business administrator, and more are pursuing degrees in administration. Progress is slow but steady. It is exciting to see! By virtue of the rising number of women among its membership, the National Church Business Administrators Association can attest to the fact that the gift of administration is, after all, not gender exclusive.

Furthermore, there are those among us who are stepping out to found ministries, establish churches, train future leaders and develop mentoring programs for women. Opportunities to lead are coming faster than we are ready to fill them.

In Concert

Our gifts work best in concert with the gifts of other believers. We not only support one another, but we also learn from one another, growing stronger in areas where we had been previously weak. There is great need for us to balance each other. For example:

- The *exhorter's* concern for a believer's maturity is balanced by the *evangelist's* love for the lost.

- The *evangelist's* cry for repentance is balanced by the *pastor's* nurturing manner.

- The *prophet's* warnings are balanced by the *mercy person's* grace.

- The *administrator's* passion for corporate success is balanced by the *server's* simple focus on others' needs.

- The *pastor's* patience is balanced by the *prophet's* blunt challenge for purity.

- The *counselor's* empathy for suffering is balanced by the *healer's* faith for a miracle.

- The *visionary's* zeal is balanced by the *administrator's* call for responsibility.

- The *teacher's* love for study is balanced by the *counselor's* desire for personal growth.

Effective ministry in the new millennium will be done in tandem with others—in teams and through networks of men and women who promote and empower one another as God leads.

TRUSTING GOD

We must not worry about the time that will be required for the vision to come to pass. Time doesn't mean to God what it does to us. In the past we may have buried our gifts, believing that because of circumstances or choices we had made, we wouldn't be able to use them. But God hasn't for a moment forgotten them—or us. He heard our hearts' cry, and He will answer—because He loves us. It was He who put the dreams in our hearts in the first place! (See John 15:16.)

When the time comes to use our gifts to help strike a chord in the Symphony, we must remember not to take credit for them. Gifts are just that—gifts. They would be called medals or trophies if we had earned them through our own great heroics.

God gives us gifts to use for the building up and equipping of others in the body and for winning the lost to Him. They are the tools of our trade; we didn't buy them or earn them, nor do we own them or take credit for what they do. We simply use what is in our hands for the glory of God. We handle the gifts as stewards, conscious always that they were designed by God Himself and must be held in pure hands.

As we serve the body of Christ with our gifts, we must leave the results up to God. He will conduct the music, and He alone has the right to take a bow.

GOING DEEPER

1. Draw a word picture of your vision—what can you see with your spiritual eyes that God wants you to be or do with your life?

2. What event or spiritual experience ignited your passion for a particular kind of ministry? Does your vision come directly out of that passion?

3. Take a spiritual gifts test and list your gifts in order of strength. What are your three strongest spiritual gifts? Your two weakest?

4. To what degree are your gifts and talents submitted to Christ's lordship?

5. How do you handle praise from others when you minister with excellence?

6. If you feel called to preach and your denomination frowns upon women preachers, what will you do about your calling? If that is not your calling, what advice would you give another woman who finds herself in such a situation?

7. How do you answer those who say women must not teach men based on 1 Timothy 2:12?

Prayer of Commitment for Today:

_____

_____

_____

_____

_____

_____

_____

_____

_____

_____

_____

3

*3
✤*

Tempo and Timing

*Teach us to number our days aright, that we may
gain a heart of wisdom.*

—PSALM 90:12

As passion, vision and gifting converge, God will bring us
to the place where we accept His timing for everything.
He will not rush; He will teach us to walk in step with Him
one day at a time before releasing us.

Curiously, God will not take us to a distant place where it
would be very obvious that we are in training. No, He will
use that which is at hand to make us grow up.

What is "at hand" in our lives right now?

Discerning God's Timing

Jenny bolted upright in bed. She glanced at the clock on her nightstand: 2:35 A.M. Across the hall, only fifteen feet away, her three-year-old was crying again.

Fatigue dogging her, Jenny pushed back the covers wearily and slid out of the bed for the fourth time that night to comfort Mary and help her through yet another vomiting incident.

"Why does the flu always strike in the middle of the night?" Jenny muttered to herself as she snapped on the hall light and opened Mary's door just enough to squeeze through, careful not to let the shaft of light strike Mary as she lay moaning in the semidarkness.

This time only dry heaves wretched Mary's little frame. "Well, it's almost over," Jenny sighed wordlessly. As she bathed Mary's face with cool water and held her close, the old feelings of resentment began to rise.

When would life consist of more than jumping up whenever the kids called and endless loads of laundry? When would there be time to read something of her choice—something a little more challenging than *Green Eggs and Ham* or *Tubby the Tugboat?* When would *she* have something to say about what she did each day and how many hours she would get to sleep at night?

Visions of teaching Bible at the college level were growing dimmer by the day. She thought of her master's degree hanging on the wall gathering dust. Oh well, given a few more years of conversing primarily with preschoolers, her vocabulary would be so depleted no administrator in his or her right mind would hire her anyway!

Jenny's attention snapped back to Mary as her daughter's arms reached up for a good-night hug. She enfolded Mary in a bear hug and then gently cuddled her, stroking her hair over and over.

"Lord, heal this little sweetheart and let us both get some rest," she weakly whispered.

Back in bed, Bill's hand reached over to hold hers. "Everything all right, Honey?" he mumbled, half asleep.

"Sure," she sighed as she pulled the covers up once more and turned on her side to sleep.

But sleep wouldn't come.

Suddenly, God spoke into her spirit: "Jenny, will you give Me ten years of your life to pass on to your children? Just ten years? Is that too much to ask of you after all the blessings I have freely given you through the years?"

Suddenly Jenny was deeply convicted about all the griping she had been doing and about the insidious resentment and discontentment that she had been nursing recently. The Holy Spirit began to show her that the "losses" were so small and temporary—that the cost of motherhood was nothing compared with the joy of loving her two little ones and watching in wonder as they grew before her very eyes!

"All right, Lord," Jenny whispered. "I think I understand. Please take these next ten years; I give them to You with no strings attached. They are Yours and theirs. Thank You for the great times—and the rough times, Lord.

"And Lord, thank You for my life—whatever it is and whatever it will become. Please don't let me waste these days in selfishness. You have been so good to me..." Her whispers trailed off into silence as she peacefully fell asleep.

PARENTING AND MINISTRY

There is a great army of women, seasoned in the fires of difficult marriages or family tragedies, that is now emerging to lead younger women through the land-mined battlefield of life. Bible teachers like Joyce Meyers and humorists like Barbara Johnson, as well as the women who speak at the tremendously popular Joyful Journey Women's Conferences, have lived life in the trenches and have come out in victory to cheer the rest of us on. They have raised their families and supported their husbands for many years, and now they have been released to bless the body of Christ in a powerful way. Their messages were learned in the waiting.

But is it possible to be in public ministry even *while* the children are growing up? In my case, after I surrendered my rights to design my days and pursue my own professional dreams much as Jenny did, God surprised me and opened the door for part-time teaching at Teen Challenge. By then, our son was in school and our daughter was old enough to go with me. As they grew, my hours at the Center increased, but I was always able to be home when they were home.

Other mothers find that their husbands will gladly pick up

the slack so that they can be involved to some degree in ministry while raising children. The attitude in our country has improved in one aspect: Finally it is acceptable, even laudable, for fathers to be deeply involved in their children's upbringing. It is recognized now that nurturing is not gender specific. In fact, for the first time perhaps, Christians are noticing that many of the images of God in the Old Testament—and of Jesus in the New Testament—are those of nurturing and "mothering" parents of spiritual children.

As the enemy's lies of the "macho man" are dispelled, men are entering into the lives of their children, blessing and being blessed enormously in return. Many fathers are finding the joy and satisfaction of instructing, comforting, listening to and caring for their children, thus releasing their wives to pursue ministry callings!

TEAMWORK

Janice and her husband, Stan, both ordained ministers, copastor a bustling church in Pennsylvania. Since their children are top priority to them, they have worked out a plan that allows them both time at home during the day. He carries 60 percent of the ministry responsibilities and 40 percent of the child-care responsibilities, and Ruth does the reverse. She finds, however, that she must guard the 60 percent with the children, because the demands of a growing congregation can easily press her to give more time than planned. On the whole, however, it is working very well.

Sometimes pastors' wives—whether ordained or not—are expected to minister in the church regardless of their children's ages or the call of God on their lives. If they are asked to put the church before their children, it can easily become a great point of stress in the home and marriage. It is critical for women to learn to hear from God for themselves, making choices free from the manipulation of others. It is important to know what we have been called by God to do, and to be able to say *no* to the rest without feeling guilty about it. Our husbands must stand behind us. If we, and they, respect our convictions and priorities, the people will come to respect them as well.

SINGLE MOMS AND MINISTRY

Angela—a single mother and an ordained evangelist—crisscrosses the United States speaking in churches and conferences while homeschooling her two children on the road. Having left an abusive husband many years ago, the Lord has healed and restored her and called her into ministry. She is under the covering of her home church and its board, and she receives their counsel gratefully. Life on the road is exhausting, but God has protected and strengthened her and placed a great anointing on her preaching. She is an unusual case, but demonstrates the resourcefulness of God. Such a life is not for the fainthearted or uncounseled or unadvised woman!

But even in the midst of raising her children by herself and pursuing full-time ministry, she echoes the warning: *If we lose our children through neglect, even to ministry, we lose not only the battle, but the war—and the world.* The constant struggle is to minister to her children first.

DON'T WASTE SINGLENESS

It is easy when we are single to become focused upon our "aloneness," but this is a grave mistake. What tremendous ministry is lost when single women think they are somehow incomplete without a husband! Was Jesus incomplete or inadequate because He wasn't married? Wasn't the key to His effectiveness the fact that He did only what the Father told Him to do? Couldn't we be effective for the same reason?

We are entering a period in our country's history that may contain the same spiritual stress that Paul and the early church experienced. Persecution may be on the way.

Whether it is imminent or not, this is a time when singleness can be a great blessing. The ease of mobility when there is only one to relocate, the undistracted attention that we can give far into the night in study and meditation, the ability to yield undivided devotion to a ministry task, the physically challenging areas that we can enter and the dangers we can face because we have no children to worry about—all these are the same reasons that Paul enjoined singles to remain in that state during those spiritually stressful times.

Settle Issues From the Past

Married or single, we can use this time to settle issues from the past. If we are in conflict with anyone in our family—especially our parents—we must go and make peace. As long as there is anger toward them, our spirits will suffer and we will be unable to see clearly our way (Prov. 20:20).

If we fear rejection, there is likely someone whom we must forgive—perhaps from long ago. If we have developed habits of procrastination, fiscal irresponsibility, people pleasing, insincerity or personal carelessness, repentance must take place and new patterns be built. If we are weak Christians, we must find mature believers of the same sex who are willing to mentor or disciple us.

Time to Prepare

We need to ask God for a vision of the task He has for us, then actively prepare for that task. If it requires going to college or Bible school, we must go, no matter how long it has been since we were in a classroom. We need not be afraid; older students are usually the curve setters of the class because they have greater focus and determination! We will probably learn more effectively than when we were kids.

The Discipline of Waiting

No matter what our situation, before we are ready to minister, we must learn to be faithful and diligent at whatever is at hand in our lives right now. As we yield our expectations and demands and find contentment in God's love for us, He will begin to send opportunities for us to minister to others. We must not despise the days of "small beginnings." He is not in a hurry. We must not become impatient and let our spiritual vision outstrip our emotional growth.

It's interesting that we feel deprived only when we think we are owed something and don't have it. Contentment comes when whatever we have is viewed as a gift from the Father's loving hands. There is no longing for what doesn't exist, because our love and energy are expended on what is at hand. Meaning can be found in simple service while we are waiting in the educational preparation or in the establishing of our own integrity and selflessness among our loved ones.

Even when we think that our spiritual giftings and passion are being neglected in favor of the "commonplace"—that which is at hand—in reality they are being disciplined and trained for greater effectiveness later.

Basic qualities of leadership are developed in the commonplace: loving and honoring others; practicing hospitality; teaching; organizing our time so as to allow care of ourselves and time in the Word and prayer; learning to work in harness with others; resolving conflict effectively on a daily basis; being mentored as well as mentoring those younger in the faith as time goes on.

TEMPERED PASSION

Passion and fire of spirit need to be tempered by self-control. If the fire in our bones for ministry does not yield first to unselfish, unheralded service to those immediately around us—most often our families and friends—it will scorch the earth rather than warm it. If this happens, in the end we will be most miserable—having damaged the cause of Christ through unbridled zeal and having alienated our loved ones in the process. We will find ourselves alone, companioned only by devouring bitterness and self-pity.

CHARACTER FIRST

It is so critical that we grasp the significance of the seasons of our lives, the different periods during which God is building character! No matter how clearly we visualize the dreams for ministry, without the graceful bowing to self-denial and a deepened sense of our own need for Christ, which teaches us how to forgive, without learning to say we are sorry to those with whom we live, there is no true ministry. Oh, we may run about doing amazing things in the name of ministry, but we will not find God in any of our efforts. No eternal effect comes without the catalyst of character, and character is built by godly responses to the things at hand.

Faithfulness—that attribute of God from which *we* have gained supremely—constitutes the fabric that must be woven into our own lives as we are dressed to carry the cross to the world. And faithfulness to those closest to us—our parents, husbands, children and friends—will be the garment that protects our hearts on the battlefield.

As we yield the timing and tempo of our lives and ministries to the Maestro, we will be given divine tutoring for the Symphony later on.

Going Deeper

1. Knowing your personal level of passion for what you feel God has called you to do in the kingdom, how have you felt "ignored" by those who could facilitate your ministering in the body of Christ and the world?

2. What is the benefit of seasons of obscurity? Can you identify any in your life? Of what specific value are they?

3. How does your family feel about your calling? Do you value their opinions and convictions? In what ways can you continue to honor your family in spite of differences, if any?

4. Are you currently being pressured to minister beyond your capacity or calling in order to meet someone else's expectations? If so, what decisions must you make?

5. How well-organized is your life? Are you occupied with needless activities that sap your energy for meaningful ministry or preparation for ministry?

6. If you are single, have you seen fresh blessing in remaining so?

7. If you are married, what is "at hand" to which you are to be faithful?

Prayer of Commitment for Today:

Part Two

Pain: Trying to Sound a Clear Note

The long summer days dragged on for Enoch. Not that his labor in the fields was anything but pleasure for him, for he was a man of the soil. To plant seed in the spring and then battle the elements to the war's glorious climax at harvest was a challenge on which he thrived. How he loved farming!

No, it really wasn't the days that dragged on, but the evenings.

"Enoch, it's getting late! How's the sermon for Sunday coming along? I'd love to hear what you're thinking about and what God is showing you. Want to talk about it?" Janet gently prodded her tired husband as she brushed the sun-bleached hair from his tanned forehead.

His shoulders heaved a bit under a deep sigh as he rubbed his eyes, put on his glasses and pulled his worn black Bible across the table. Idly thumbing the pages, he sighed again.

"I don't think I'm hearing anything from God!" Enoch groaned. "Sometimes that really scares me, Janet. I love God and respect His Word, but I'm just not cut out to preach. I'll never understand why the church chose me!"

Janet reached into the refrigerator for the

lemonade pitcher and filled a tall glass for him, quickly adding ice cubes to keep it cold.

"I believe in you, Enoch, and so do the people. We know how sincere and honest you are, and that alone teaches us volumes. Just always tell the truth about God, and we will grow. Besides, I'll help you get the sermon ready. We're a team, you know!"

Her voice became even softer as she took his calloused hand in hers. "Let's ask Him right now what the people need to hear on Sunday. Then we'll look through the Word together. I know He'll speak to us!"

Enoch gratefully bowed his head, and they took turns talking to the Lord. As the sunset faded from the horizon, the Lord began revealing His thoughts to them, and Janet, pen and paper in hand, began writing them down, thought by thought, verse by verse.

4

❧

Playing Second Fiddle

This is what the LORD says: "Restrain your voice from weeping and your eyes from tears, for your work will be rewarded," declares the LORD.

—JEREMIAH 31:16

I t is rarely the world that breaks the hearts of women in ministry, but rather those within the household of faith who bring us pain. When we are treated poorly by the world, we take it in stride; we don't expect them to understand our call. But when those in the church neglect or belittle us as we seek to obey God, the hurt goes deep.

Two for the Price of One

Their interview at Lakeside Community Church was going well. Mary was excited—maybe even more than Jim! Lakeside Community not only needed a senior pastor, but they also needed to replace their music director, who had recently left.

Mary had forwarded her application for the position of music director shortly after Jim had applied for the pastorate. With her qualifications and exceptional performance at their last church, it seemed like a perfect match. How like God!

And how they needed the extra income! The cost of living in New York was going to be higher than what it had been in Louisiana, where they had lived before. The music director's salary of $13,000 a year plus Jim's would be a tremendous blessing. As the interview ended, they rose to shake hands with each member of the search committee.

"You will receive a letter from us with our decision within two weeks," the chairman stated with a big grin. "You both come highly recommended, and the Holy Spirit has obviously gifted you in your areas of ministry. It's been a delight getting to know you!"

"Sounds good so far, doesn't it, Hon?" Jim whispered into her ear as he held open the car door for her in the church parking lot.

She turned to kiss his cheek just before slipping into her seat. "And I won't have to look for a job somewhere else. We can work together!"

Just five days later the confirmation from the search committee arrived. They were both unanimously approved! They quickly read each paragraph, eagerly devouring every word.

But when their eyes reached the salary figure at the bottom of the page, Mary's heart nearly stopped. A mere $1,000 was tacked onto Jim's salary to cover her ministry.

"Two for the price of one," Jim mumbled numbly.

"How could they think of taking advantage of me this way?" Mary cried. "I'm not just an appendage to you! I've worked hard and served faithfully for years in the church with my gifts. I deserve to be paid what they would have paid anyone else. I'm so hurt and angry, Jim! Hasn't the church gotten beyond seeing women as able only to 'play second fiddle' yet?"

Jim pulled Mary into his arms, letting the letter drift to the floor. The breeze from an open window blew it across the room and into a corner. She sighed heavily as she leaned into his shoulder.

"We need to seek God, Mary. Maybe this isn't the place for us after all," he said softly. "I didn't expect this double standard from them. The world would have treated you better than this! I know that in the past this was common in the ministry, but I thought the church had finally grown beyond such insensitivity."

They sank to their knees right there, Jim still holding Mary as she tried not to cry. Slowly she opened her heart to God.

"Lord, I really am so disappointed! I really believe that a workman deserves his wages as Your Word says, and I don't understand this. Help me fight the temptation to turn bitter!

Keep me sweet, Lord, and from feeling second rate. Show me Your hand in this." She heaved a sigh. "I forgive them, and I ask You to forgive them, too."

After a long pause, she continued slowly, "And Lord, if You want me to serve here under these conditions, I'll do it, even if I don't understand how we can make ends meet. I just want to be obedient to You, Lord."

Jim cleared his throat and stroked her hand lovingly. "Lord, show us what to do. What is Your will for us right now?"

END OF STORY

Mary and Jim heard God tell them to serve as unto Him, and He would reward Mary Himself. She obediently gave her best unto the Lord, expanding the choir ministry from two choirs to five, taking three of them on tour. She also wrote and directed Christmas and Easter musicals that brought honor to the Lord and to the church.

And Mary discovered a hidden blessing in not being paid for all her work: She had the freedom to take time off to develop her own musical talents and spiritual gifts. As she branched out in her ministry to the body of Christ—cohosting a Christian TV show, cutting records and leading worship at international conferences—God began fine-tuning His call on her life.

Mary is now taking an Easter musical she wrote while at that church to other countries where it has become a powerful tool for evangelism! She also conducts international prayer and worship seminars, leading and ministering in her own right, esteemed and respected wherever she goes.

OTHER TIMES

Sometimes the story doesn't end so neatly. Sometimes everyone loses.

Susan was an exuberant, intelligent, creative worker who served for many years in the public service department of a well-known parachurch ministry in the Northeast. She was gifted administratively and was instrumental in bringing many very important innovations to the department, enhancing the ministry's image to the public and improving the service to staff within the ministry. Susan had been hired as a secretary, but she had quickly proven her managerial and leadership ability and had become the indispensable right hand of the director of the department. She was generally perceived to be the more decisive, organized and visionary of the two.

When the director retired, Susan (and most of the staff) felt that no better replacement could be found than she. Susan had earned the position, and since her husband was an invalid, the increase in pay would financially reward her for her many years of faithful effectiveness.

However, the board members and the ministry's executives acted as though she didn't exist. They seemed "stuck" in seeing her only as a helper. They brought in a former pastor who had no prior experience in parachurch public relations and was not gifted as a leader or administrator. But apparently because he had been a pastor, as had been most of the other executives in the ministry, he was given the job. But it was obvious to all the staff in "the ranks" that they had made a big mistake.

After a spiritual wrestling match with her disappointment, Susan forgave, but she didn't stay. She had been offered an administrative position in a large area business. Because she needed greater income due to her husband's deteriorating health, she took the position, even though it broke her heart to leave the work and people she loved. Her leaving was a great loss to the ministry and a real blow to a gifted woman of God who had given so much to that organization.

Fortunately, she was too deeply in love with the Lord and the body of Christ to get bitter, but it must have been a difficult sadness to overcome.

FEELING INVISIBLE

I have *almost* become accustomed to being seemingly invisible in the male ministry marketplace. My husband, however, has wrestled with indignation at times over the neglect he has perceived me receiving. While I don't want him to ever become bitter or doubt God's goodness to me, his confidence in me has blessed me greatly! How wonderful it is to have someone—especially a man, and one who knows me well—believe in me and what God has called me to do in training men and women in ministry leadership. He gets no end of pleasure when men view me first by the spirit, not concerned about my gender.

And there are other men out there like that. I am meeting them one by one. I have come to trust God to give me divine encounters with them—and it is happening!

PLAYING CATCH-UP

The body of Christ is slowly coming out of its presumptuous treatment of women. Changes in our culture have forced everyone to think twice before openly devaluing women.

Sadly, it seems to take the influence of the world to bring reform in the body of Christ. The church's own initiatives usually trail five to ten years behind those of secular culture. It is embarrassing that the world has had to take the lead in exposing the sins of racial prejudice and sexual abuse—and now gender injustice—but it is horrible that vast numbers within the church have found the same sins within their own hearts and lives! Has the church in the past been too busy hiding her problems in order to protect her reputation and too proud to face the blight in her very midst?

Perhaps more than that, hesitancy has been rooted in the fact that church leaders typically spend much of their time looking backward, working to stabilize themselves on the last move of God. Often they forget to ask for a fresh revelation of their own condition.

The body of Christ in this country leaves it up to the world to break new ground, but then, because men and women alike are suspicious of what the world is up to, we retreat even further. We don't act until we are absolutely forced to correct the injustices.

INTEGRITY BY EXAMPLE

The church should *model integrity,* taking the lead in honoring men and women equally. If we did, the world would truly take notice! If repentance and intentional reform were to occur in earnest, a ripple effect would begin throughout our culture, bringing reform of a *lasting, healing* nature.

The world's reforms will never do the job. Typical of Satan's actions, they are based upon half-truths. Yes, there is injustice and something must be done. But because secular reforms aren't capable of changing the *hearts* of men, one "reform" often leads to another problem.

How can we hang back when we have the answer to the injustices in society? How can we remain insecure and divided among ourselves, elevating men and devaluing women in most quarters when we know Christ's view of us? When are we going to take Him and one another seriously?

Until the climate changes throughout the body of Christ, God may ask us to choose to risk hurt in order to model vulnerability and our commitment to a higher call, retaining a heart for the people regardless of how we are treated. How tragic if we choose instead to build walls around our hearts, keeping at a distance the very people to whom God desires we minister, in an attempt to avoid disappointment and pain—or worse still, if we choose to abandon the call!

OUR RESPONSE

As we reflect on the roles that women play in our churches and ministries, let's encourage reform. Are they being treated fairly based on their competencies, accomplishments and character? If we can bring continuing change within the church, let's have the courage to do it. At the very least, let's freely express our appreciation to women personally, honestly and often.

And if we ourselves have been "used" by Christian organizations or have spent our lives playing "second fiddle" when the quality of our work should have placed us in a lead position, let's forgive and go on in obedience to the Maestro. He sees our situation and will use it to give us a much-needed ministry of grace to other Christians who often miss the anointing that accompanies humility.

If we can keep our eyes fixed on Him and our ears tuned to the words of affirmation that *He* whispers to us, we *will* become instruments for His glory.

1. Describe the spiritual attributes of any men who have encouraged your calling.

2. There are many wonderful books on the market now addressing women's place in ministry. How are many theologians now defending in writing women's right to minister as God calls?

3. Have you ever been ridiculed for pursuing the call to minister that you heard from God? If so, have you forgiven the offenders? Why is it important to forgive, even if you are right and they are wrong?

4. What emotions would you feel if a less-qualified man were promoted over you in ministry?

5. If you felt you were being kept in a "second fiddle" position, what scriptures could keep you at rest and enable you to make wise decisions?

6. How can the church model integrity in the area of women in ministry? What practical steps could you take in your own sphere of influence to model integrity?

7. How can you personally encourage women of integrity in the ministry who are struggling with the issue of their role in ministry?

Prayer of Commitment for Today:

5

❧

Qualified to Play in the Symphony

You did not choose me, but I chose and appointed you to go and bear fruit—fruit that will last.

—JOHN 15:16

The call to pastor is being heard and answered by an increasing number of women. Our commitment must be rock solid and our ability to hear from God beyond question if we are to overcome the obstacles ahead.

TRYING TO PROVE OUR WORTH

The massive oak door—supported by great wrought iron

53

hinges that spread their fingers halfway across the door at its top and bottom—gave way to Nancy's push. Worn by generations of students' comings and goings, it moved with ease under even this slight seminarian's touch.

As she slid into the wooden chair just inside the classroom door and adjusted the desk before her, Nancy's eye caught the flash of Jonathan's smile from two aisles over. They were both in the class of '98, headed hopefully for pulpits somewhere in the United States.

She had learned so much from Jonathan. Unlike many of the men, he wasn't resentful of her presence in the seminary—afraid that she would take the place due him or convinced of her inadequacy in presenting the Word with authority. No, he treated her as an equal, seeing beyond her gender to her spirit, feeling at home with her as he came to know the purity of her pursuit of God.

"Ready to get your grade on that 'monster' exam we took last week?" He spoke softly behind the back of his hand so as not to be heard by the professor who was taking his place at the podium as a hush fell upon the room.

All she could do in the ensuing silence was give him a half-grin, twisting her bottom lip to the side and rolling her eyes. He almost laughed aloud at her contortions! It had been a killer of a test, and he knew that a great deal rode on the results. If they were to continue at the seminary, this was a hurdle that must be overcome.

As though apologizing for her response to him, she pointed to heaven—which brought a quick smile to Jonathan's face. He nodded in return. They both knew that their destinies lay in God's hands—and pointing toward heaven was their silent signal to remind each other of that fact.

Across the room, edgy and uncomfortable, Gloria stiffly awaited her grade. She was sure that every man in the room hoped for her demise! She had pushed herself relentlessly ever since arriving, convinced that she had to score higher than any of the men to prove herself in this male-dominated profession.

Nothing less than an A was enough; under the strain to be perfect, she had almost broken last semester. But the fear of facing in failure the presbytery that had endorsed her drove her to regroup, to pull herself together by sheer force. But always she felt unworthy and imagined others' like-judgment of her.

Nancy and Jonathan had recently begun praying for her, detecting her struggle with perfectionism and her fear of rejection. They prayed that she would come to see her own spiritual value and God's signature upon her life. They knew that if Gloria was to succeed, she needed a word from God—and the humility to believe that word and die to her pride in order to be obedient. She needed to find her confidence in God.

VALIDITY ESTABLISHED BY GOD

If God has called us to pastor, no amount of prejudice can ever disqualify us in His sight.

If we fall into measuring our validity by the same standard used by those who oppose us, we will get into competitiveness as we try to prove our worthiness. And in so doing, we will be scorning the fully sufficient endorsement of the Holy Spirit upon our call. How sad and wasteful of peace it is to disbelieve His divine approval and spend all our emotional energy trying to persuade others!

As Nancy and Jonathan continued to pray, God began to speak into Gloria's heart. He reassured her of His love and plan for her life and reminded her to fix her eyes on Jesus. As she did, she was able to release others' judgments of her to God.

It finally dawned upon her that her heavenly Father would be her champion! If anyone else had a wrong attitude toward her, God would deal with it. It was not her job to convince them of anything! When she detected disapproval, she would learn to ask the Lord to keep her spirit sweet and gracious, remembering that Jesus had suffered such antagonism ahead of her—yet had remained loving and set in His purpose.

Strangely, as she grew into a deeper walk of confidence in Christ, more and more of the male students began showing respect for her! Even though some never could accept her as a prospective pastor—professors included—by the time she graduated, many others were cheering her on.

This is a lesson that is best learned early, because prejudice will not end at graduation from seminary or Bible school—or at ordination. At times, men who are less qualified will be promoted instead of us. We will be paid less to speak at conferences than men with the same credentials. We will be patted on the head by some and told to be content to remain in support roles, when we know that God has prepared us and called us to leadership. Some may even tell us that we are in rebellion to the very One whom we are trying to obey!

There will be as many ways to be intentionally or unintentionally slighted as there are people on this earth! But if we remember that judgment is God's—just as the call on our lives came from God—we will keep our eyes fixed on His approval alone and remain sweet in spirit. Our integrity will be our protection.

STIGMA PRIMARILY CULTURAL

One way that we know the stigma against women pastoring in this country is primarily cultural is that critics' views change when we decide to minister in a foreign country. Suddenly everyone relaxes and wishes us well! In a seminar recently the main speaker made an interesting statement: "It seems that the only audience to which a woman is not qualified to preach is one that is male, white, middle class and American!"

For some reason our obeying God in any role on the mission field poses no problems for even the most conservative Christian. It's when we come home that the restrictions begin.

HOME FROM THE MISSION FIELD

Lindy leaned forward in her seat, stretching to catch a glimpse of the ground as the plane descended to ten thousand feet above the airport in Wheeling, West Virginia. So many buildings, streets and homes! As always, its size, compared to that of the little villages in Tanzania, struck her with force as she returned home once more.

But this time was different. She was coming home to stay. After thirty years in Africa—preaching the gospel, discipling men and women in the Word, building churches and raising up indigenous pastors to lead flocks of their own—Lindy felt a deep hunger to return to the States to minister to her own countrymen. Her dream was to be sent out by her home church to build new congregations in the rural areas of West Virginia, much as she had in Africa.

"Please prepare for landing by fastening your seatbelts and returning your seats to an upright position," the pilot intoned over the intercom.

Her heart beat more rapidly. Reverend Johnson and his wife, Meredith, would be there to meet her. Would they be as excited about her plans as she was?

As the plane taxied to a stop, she gathered her carry-on from under the seat. At the sound of the chime signifying the completed landing, she hurriedly unbuckled her seatbelt and stood so as to exit the plane as soon as possible.

"Lindy! How wonderful to have you home!" Meredith hugged her warmly as she came out of Gate 9 and into the waiting room. "You must be exhausted!"

"Not really. That plane ride was pure luxury compared to my usual mode of transportation in the bush of Tanzania!" laughed Lindy. "I'm not used to padded seats, air conditioning and stewardesses serving refreshments!"

At this they all laughed. Reverend Johnson helped her pull her luggage off the conveyor belt in the baggage claim area.

Later, as they got settled in the Johnsons' car, Lindy happily shared about the call God had placed on her heart for planting churches in the country. She knew it would take time, but if the whole church could catch the vision, plans could be in place in perhaps six months to begin preaching in some of the more remote areas.

Reverend and Mrs. Johnson were quiet. After Lindy was "talked out," the pastor cleared his throat.

He began to speak cautiously. "Lindy, do you really think that it is proper for a single lady to be running around the countryside preaching, especially to men? It doesn't seem right—or safe—does it?"

"A lot safer and just as proper as doing it in Africa!" Lindy laughed, expecting them to join her in seeing the humor of the conversation.

But they didn't laugh. "We have plenty for you to do at the church. We'd like you to teach the third graders in Sunday school and perhaps start a women's Bible study on Wednesday nights. In fact, we could use your help printing the bulletins each week."

Now it was Lindy's turn to be quiet. She was stunned. For thirty years she had been preaching and evangelizing, and God had not told her to stop in order to print bulletins! There were lost and unchurched men and women in West Virginia just as there were in Africa, and she had learned through long years of experience how to share the gospel effectively with such people and bring them into body ministry with each other. That was the call of God on her life!

"Well, you can tell the folks at church all about your mission adventures on Sunday night in the Fellowship Hall. Did you bring along artifacts and slides to show us?" Reverend Johnson countered, in a weak attempt to change the subject.

DOUBLE STANDARD

This embarrassing double standard prevails in many denominations. Leaders in the churches where this exists would do well to come to grips with such inconsistencies and ask forgiveness of women pastors and missionaries who have been treated with condescension. If only they could see that their reservations have been cultural, not spiritual, and that if they had asked, "What would Jesus do?" their conventions would have been blown to bits!

SOMEDAY

When the Symphony assembles, gender will not matter. Qualifying factors will be then as they should have been all along: a holy, disciplined and temperate life; order in our homes; faithfulness to our spouses and families; willingness to entertain strangers without selfishness; a good reputation in our communities and a propensity for teaching the Word to others.

That we are instruments for His glory—playing our parts with faithfulness and humility—will be what brings down the house on opening night.

GOING DEEPER

1. What scriptures can you use to defend the right of women to pastor?

2. Do you think that women have had to be more highly trained and gifted than men when competing for pastoral assignments?

3. How can women avoid developing a competition mentality about their role in ministry beside men?

4. In what ways could a woman be strengthened through opposition?

5. What will qualify you to serve where God has called you?

7. What double standards have you experienced in the church? Do you practice any yourself?

Prayer of Commitment for Today:

_____

_____

_____

_____

_____

_____

_____

_____

_____

_____

6

❦

Finding
the Right Pitch

Stop judging by mere appearances, and make a right judgment.

—JOHN 7:24

Even when we women are given the freedom to act within our giftings, even when we know that the Word supports the call, we often "shoot ourselves in the foot" because we aren't convinced of our own position and responsibility in Christ.

It's with some embarrassment that I recall such a "foot-shooting" incident in my own life that occurred while I was teaching at an all-male Christian drug and alcohol rehabilitation ministry several years ago.

FEAR OF MAN

The day dawned bright and clear, a perfect Sunday morning. I rose and quickly dressed for church—remembering to wear flat-heeled shoes for easy walking in grassy, hilly terrain. I would be helping to serve communion at the outdoor Jesus Celebration over at "God's Mountain"—what we affectionately called the Teen Challenge Training Center, situated in the hills of Pennsylvania. Each year at the climax of the festive weekend, hundreds of alumni and guests, the entire student body of nearly two hundred fifty men and the staff take communion together—and this year it was the academic division's turn to serve the elements. I had waited several years for it to be our turn and was very excited about serving the Lord and my fellow believers in this simple but extremely significant way.

When I arrived at the Celebration site, I parked the car and quickly walked to the tent where we were to receive our instructions from the center director. When I entered the large, brown canvas counseling tent, the other teachers were just forming a circle to pray. One or two of the men glanced my way but said nothing, then turned back to face the center of the circle.

I froze. *What was I doing here?* Suddenly the fact that I was the only woman teacher seemed like an immensely significant fact. While working alongside these men day after day for sixteen years, I had given little conscious thought to the "male-female thing" as far as fulfilling my responsibilities to the students and God was concerned. We had all become comrades for the gospel's sake.

But as I faced all these men's backs and bowed heads and felt the seriousness of the moment, I imagined that they were uncomfortable with my being there—that somehow I didn't belong because I was a woman!

I burned with embarrassment and confusion. Quickly I turned on my heels and ran out of the tent and up the grassy slope to the treeline that ringed the crest of the hill. Sinking to the ground, I fought back tears as I frantically ran a mental check over all the New Testament scriptures I could recall in an effort to discover my error. But for the life of me, I couldn't think of a single scripture that prevented women from serving the communion elements.

My mind raced. *Why had my friends been so distant? Why hadn't they opened the circle to invite me in? What had I done wrong? If it was against the rules of the denomination, why hadn't they had the kindness to tell me so before I showed up and made an idiot of myself? And why was the church so sexist anyway?* By this time I was becoming self-righteously indignant.

The next day during one of my classes, I received a call from Sonny, the center director. He asked me to come to his office as soon as that class was over.

As I knocked at the door of his office a few minutes later, he called out, "Come on in, Joyce." I couldn't tell by his voice what was up. As I entered, he flashed me a warm smile and waved me to one of the chairs in front of his desk. This was a man for whom I had great respect, who had always acted in my best interest throughout the years.

He got right to the point. "Why did you leave the tent yesterday?"

Startled, I clumsily replied, "I didn't think you men wanted me there! I was embarrassed and took off..." My gaze fell to the floor for a moment and then returned to his face.

"Did we say that we didn't want you there?" he softly asked, looking straight at me.

"Well no, but no one moved to let me join the circle."

"Joyce, most of the men didn't even see you come in. Before those who did see you could think to move, you were gone!" Sonny explained with a touch of frustration in his voice.

"I thought maybe some church doctrine prohibited my participation—and I just didn't know it," I added lamely.

"Does Scripture prohibit it?" he pressed.

"No." I was beginning to feel very foolish.

"Then you should have stayed. And even if any of them *had* been uncomfortable, that would have been *their* problem, not *yours*. Do you understand?" he probed gently.

Silence fell on the room. Then he continued, "Joyce, you need to know who you are in Christ, especially if you are going to work here. Next time something like this happens, even if you are truly being discriminated against, simply stay. If you have a question, ask. You are as much a part of this ministry as anyone else. Understand?"

I understood. Heaving a sigh of relief, I rose to leave. As he walked me to the door he placed his hand lightly on my shoulder, stopping me long enough to quietly say again, "Joyce, know who you are in Christ."

It was a very telling moment for me.

TEARING DOWN IDOLS

If Sonny hadn't called me in that day, the seed of bitterness that my previous perception and reaction had produced would have grown into a weed of arrogance, eventually defiling everyone I taught. My need to walk free of idolizing acceptance by man, which repeatedly made me easily intimidated, was more important to God that morning than my being invited to serve communion.

Idolatry is subtle; the idols can be crafted into a great variety of innocent-looking forms. To find the idol we must go first to the seat of our affections—our hearts—and take stock of what is most important to us. We can ask ourselves: "What would I not want to be withheld from me? The absence of what ingredient would make ministry not satisfying to me anymore?" If the answer is anything but God's presence, we have likely discovered an idol of our own crafting.

Self-Worship

I remember the time after I had spoken in chapel at Teen

Challenge that the students' pastor asked me for a copy of my notes from the message so that he could use them himself someday. My gut reaction is still so vivid that I can feel it right now many years later.

Without saying it aloud, down in my heart these words screamed: *Develop your own notes! I worked hard to put this together, and I don't want to share the credit for it with anyone else!*

How ashamed I am of those thoughts now! I've repented of the self-worship that lay behind it, and I ask the Holy Spirit to monitor my heart regularly for signs of its growth again. Self-worship, in the forms of self-protection and self-promotion, is the driving force behind our hunger for recognition, our propensity for enjoying another's failure, our judgments of those in authority and our ministry territorialism. Without the blessings of repentance and God's forgiveness, I'd not dare to be involved in ministry today—knowing myself and the sin of which I am capable!

It's interesting that before we can give our lives for the gospel's sake, we have to consent to placing our hearts under the microscope of the Holy Spirit's convicting power and be willing to haul to the cross whatever is found there that is not of God.

It seems that we won't forsake our sin until we see and understand how truly putrid it is. And God is great at engineering its exposure! If we fail to respond to His continual nudgings about something that is wrong in our lives, failing to repent, He will simply allow us to go on as our selfishness wills until we "undo" ourselves, often to the injury of many.

Finally, we lay it all on the altar. Finally, we realize that the misery in which we have been wallowing began in our own hearts.

Worship of Men

I have long been fascinated by God's words to Eve after the Fall: "Your desire will be for your husband, and he will rule over you" (Gen. 3:16). This pronouncement, contrary to public opinion, was *not* a curse. Only the ground and the serpent were cursed. This is, however, a prediction of the way in which our relationships will malfunction if our eyes are on one another rather than on God. But it is not an inevitable, irredeemable condition of the human heart.

Before Understanding Our Value

"Rulership" is given to men when we expect them to be God—to have wisdom for both of us and be infallible in their judgment—looking to them to give our lives meaning. We mistakenly think that gaining their love and acceptance will meet every need that we will ever have.

Since they know deep inside that they can never fulfill these expectations and because they are laboring under the same delusions we are, they hide their inadequacies and fears behind domination. What an uneasy throne they must mount!

And inevitably we like it no more than they. As women struggle to allow men to represent us and deliver purpose to our lives—something wrenches within us. We know instinctively that there is more to who we are than they realize. Their representation of us is insufficient, because they cannot reflect the half of God's image that we should be revealing.

Having never found our God-given identity, we feel lost. Out of this grows anger. As we demand more and become quite disconsolate, they withdraw further from us, not knowing what to do.

It's a vicious cycle. Because our desire—our longing for a lord—has been directed to men, we have given them the power to rule our lives—as well as the power to make our lives miserable! We don't realize that our inner need has been to be led by God Himself, to hear *His* words of affirmation, to be part of a family and a kingdom in which we have value on our own.

A Better Way

It is interesting that ruling and being ruled bring little joy to either men or women. From a man's point of view, to have a woman totally dependent upon him for her value, purpose and joy is a heavy burden indeed to bear—such expectations being impossible for *any* human being to fulfill on behalf of another. As a result this is *not* fertile ground in which mutual respect or deep friendship can grow.

72

It isn't that most men want women to be *in*dependent of them, but rather to be *inter*dependent—equally responsible parts of a whole, which we become together. This is borne out in marriage, body ministry and even the workplace.

As we come to know who we are in Christ, our men will be free to seek their identities in God's love and purpose for their own lives—not in ruling positions or power plays in the field of relationships. They will finally be able to relax and be themselves—children of God, seekers of truth, bearers of God's image as well as forgiven mistake-makers. There will be no thrones to guard. Colaboring will begin!

This is what should set Christians apart from the world. Our men should not need to play the roles of omniscient kings with us—they should be our comrades and friends. And instead of being tentative and insecure around them, we should expect the best—because we have turned our faces toward God. *He* will fulfill His plans for us as much as for them.

PRECIOUS COUNTERPARTS

Before the Fall, when Adam saw Eve, he saw his counterpart—a creature strangely akin to himself. God had multiplied His image from within man out and into this woman—bone of his bone, flesh of his flesh. Adam didn't have to subdue her to win her, and she didn't have to pander to him to be accepted. There was no competition, no manipulation, no domination—only pure pleasure in one another's company. This was God's intention.

When sin entered their hearts through rebellion, God's plan for colaboring under His rule was temporarily thwarted. Out of the curse—among other horrors—arose the growth of control of one sex by the other, as well as the abandonment of God's authority.

But in His love God sent His Son to break sin's curse and set the captive free. Through Jesus' death and resurrection, He restored divine order for those who would trust Him for salvation and accept His kingship over their lives in all things. Through Jesus' life and the deposit of His Holy Spirit within believers, peace was restored and His authority reestablished in the hearts of men and women of every race and culture. Therefore, even in the midst of a still-chaotic world, Paul could see with spiritual eyes into the kingdom that had come and say, "There is neither Jew nor Greek, slave nor free, male nor female, for you are all one in Christ Jesus" (Gal. 3:28). He pronounced the end of the battle of the sexes and the completeness of all in Christ. His life within us redeems what was lost by the fall (Rom. 8:1–17).

Because of what was accomplished at Calvary, we can now meet our brothers as fulfilled women, not shadows that are beholden to them for our substance. Jesus completes us by His life within ours.

THEIR DESIRE

Mature men will want us to know that our eternal purpose comes from God—not their attention or perfection. They will respect us *more* and dominate us *less* when we respect ourselves and speak truthfully and without manipulation. They are more comfortable dealing with problems that are straightforward, even if difficult, and would be relieved if we would shed ambivalence and stop hiding our true feelings behind false submission.

Few men want women to be their slaves or to act like mindless children; most want partners and coworkers with whom they can be real, even within great difficulties. They want honest relationships within which everyone can grow.

Our wholeness and confidence in Christ, our truthfulness and willingness to be responsible for our own actions would be a great blessing to them. And interestingly, *as we respect ourselves, our ability to respect them increases.* As we learn to trust God for our lives, we will be able to give them the space to be who they are and to grow at their own rate.

Meanwhile, released from our expectations, men will be free to more honestly pursue their own relationships with God and embrace *His* love for them. As they absorb His unconditional, cherishing love, they will find a greater capacity to respect and honor us!

When We Have Been Hurt

If any of us have been cruelly beaten down within relationships in years past—if we find ourselves shaking from fear that our lives are a mistake and that we are beyond usefulness and joy—we need to find the cross.

It is amazing that Scripture doesn't say to *blame* others so that we may be healed, but to *confess our sins* to one another so that we may be healed (James 5:16). For with every wound that has been inflicted upon us for any reason, if we are hurt, there has been a sinful reaction on our own part for which we are responsible. We must forgive those persons who sinned against us—setting them free from our judgment and revenge. But we must also cry out for forgiveness for having borne that judgment and revenge in our hearts for so very long.

Healing and restoration always begin at the cross, where Jesus died not only for our sins, but those committed against us. As we confess to God *and* a brother or sister, asking for Christ's forgiveness while extending that very same forgiveness to those who hurt us, we find that the poison of the injury eating away at our lives for years has disappeared! We are free! The load is off our backs and buried by His blood at Calvary. What a miracle!

New Identities

And then we suddenly *know who we are:* children of the

living God, joint heirs with Jesus of all the promises, full-fledged members of the royal priesthood, new creatures in Christ, a holy people and the bearers of the glory of God on this earth! And because we did nothing to earn all this, we won't need our names in lights or to receive credit for simply living out the grace He has bestowed on our lives.

What freedom! What preparation for the Symphony to come when we surrender once and for all to the music that transcends even the "greatest" mission here on earth! As His image is restored to our lives, we will play our instruments with perfect pitch, bringing peace to all who hear.

1. Have you ever embarrassed yourself when asked to perform some duty in ministry? Describe the scenario. What did you learn from it?

2. What idols has God revealed to you that you have crafted in your life? How can you tear them down?

3. What has the phrase *to fear man* meant personally to you?

4. What is your conviction about the rulership of men over women as predicted in Genesis 3:16?

5. What is the difference between *rulership* and *authority* when it comes to leadership?

6. Have you been sinned against, perhaps even sexually, by a man in spiritual leadership over you? If you haven't already gotten it, seek counsel for the wounds that remain so that you can enter ministry without bitterness in your heart.

7. Describe your spiritual identity in Christ. How does your identity in Christ alter your understanding of the consequence of sin as described in Genesis 3:16?

Prayer of Commitment for Today:

_____

_____

_____

_____

_____

_____

_____

_____

_____

As the sun's first rays broke between the distant rambling mountain peaks, Enoch found Janet on her knees in the spare bedroom that used to be their daughter Anna's before she died. Through Anna's illness Janet had possessed a special "knowing" that had given her husband and the other children strength.

They never really understood that "knowing," but sensed only that it came from something deep within her from God. It was as though she had a secret ability to yield everything in trust to God without anger and without demands of blessing in return.

No mother had loved her children more dearly, yet when God took Anna home, Janet's hands never grasped nor formed fists raised in the face of God. There had been tears many times—and still were—but the tears never distorted her vision of the life that still remained.

Most difficult of all, however, was the fact that Enoch's memory was failing. There were whispers among the neighbors that he had Alzheimer's disease, and Janet suspected they were right. He had been preaching for twenty-two years now, but over the last few years she had had to do more and more prompting from the front pew. He'd simply forget what he had said last. Then he'd look pleadingly at her lips until she whispered enough to put him right again.

Her heart broke for him, but she never gave him pity—she respected him too much for that. They were still a team as she had always told him, and she simply covered for him by taking care of his pastoral duties when he wasn't up to them.

The "knowing" kept her at peace through it all. The longing for public ministry rarely dogged her heart anymore, for she "knew" the character of God. She knew that His faithfulness endured forever. A deeper understanding of ministry had taken root: the life of the cross. She had never been more in love with the Lord than now, for suffering had provided yet another connection between her and Him.

After lovingly watching his wife for several minutes from the doorway as she prayed there in Anna's room, Enoch silently stepped back and closed the door.

As he strode out into the fresh morning air and headed for the barn, four words slipped softly from his lips: "I love you, Janet." He smiled and began whistling.

7

❧

Giving Up First Chair in the Symphony

On my bed I remember you; I think of you through the watches of the night. Because you are my help, I sing in the shadow of your wings. I stay close to you; your right hand upholds me.

—PSALM 63:6–8

Just as Corrie Ten Boom did in *The Hiding Place* when she found only more delays and more hardships at the very time that her release from concentration camp seemed imminent, we too wail, "Lord, how long will it take?"

And the Lord answers us as Betsie answered Corrie that day, "Perhaps a long, long time. Perhaps many years. But what better way could there be to spend our lives?"

As Corrie and Betsie entered the worst prison camp in

Germany during World War II, one from which no one was supposed to come out alive, Betsie was free—her spirit unshackled and able to embrace the situation without anger. What she saw was not barbed wire and filthy barracks, but guards whose faces were distorted with hate. Her heart broke with compassion for them instead of for herself. She saw in the spirit what Jesus saw on the cross—the desperate need of others to know the love of God.

To give to their enemies the love they so desperately needed, Jesus—and Betsie—were both willing to die. Where and under what circumstances the dying occurred wouldn't matter—the joy of offering redemption would be the same. Whether lauded or ridiculed, the course was set, and they were committed.

To allow, even invite, God's compassion and love to flow through us to others so that they see Jesus and come to Him—learning how to love instead of hate—is a divine mission. It is not defined by position or place, only by our obedience in doing what we can, right where we are, with clean hands and hearts.

Danger of Low Expectations

How I long to see the release of more godly women to preach, teach and evangelize, to function in grace and wisdom in the prophetic, to train and lead others with good sense and compassion as I know many can. I grieve that few of our male leaders comprehend the dreadful loss of effective ministry that exists when women are encouraged to expect little of themselves in the kingdom, their giftings lying dormant through neglect and ignorance.

And I am appalled that so many women are comfortable watching the world go by! I am embarrassed that we are known for our penchant for shopping rather than for our readiness to cultivate spiritual growth in the church and bring change in the world.

But I weep as well when even one of us who *has* caught the vision moves prematurely or in arrogance.

SPIRITUAL ARROGANCE

Presumption is a terrible sin and an easy one for us to commit. Men do not have a corner on that market by any means! We are a passionate crew—but sometimes passion, like a freight train gone wild, can jump its tracks and spew gravel far into the fields, wounding any living thing in its path.

Visions are wonderful gifts, I know. This book is the result of a vision God gave me fifteen years ago when I first began experiencing the struggles of ministering as a woman in all-male territory. But if I had written it then, it would have been wasted and out of kilter, for the greatest breaking of my life had not yet occurred. At that time I thought I knew everything! How amazing that today I know so little!

Resentments and Judgments

Through the years, men who were in authority over me and those who worked alongside me were, for the most part, kind and appreciative. A few were knights in shining armor for me in the early days at Teen Challenge as I learned the ropes of instructing men who came from drug and alcohol abuse backgrounds. The greatest words of advice I have ever received were given by men.

But I remember two areas of struggle: One was with those few who could relate to me only as a female—someone to be noticed and complimented for my appearance but rarely asked for an opinion or engaged in serious conversation about anything. I knew that I would be able to advance in that ministry only so far—regardless of qualification. All the leaders were men, and they could not imagine a woman being in any kind of management position.

The result was a wounding that I did not at that time know enough to forgive. Resentment, for which I thought I was justified, grew and began to defile my heart.

The other struggle was with myself as I judged their work at times and felt I could do better. Maybe I could have in some instances—if I had been given opportunity to gain more experience—but God could not allow it because of my lack of compassion and humility.

I was missing a certain settledness, that "knowing" that God was in control. In my heart I was sometimes presumptuous in my judgment calls—presumptuous in thinking my wisdom exceeded theirs or that my judgment was better than theirs.

TAKING MATTERS INTO MY OWN HANDS

It seemed so logical. Since students weren't getting the help they needed from the Counseling Department, which was overloaded with paperwork for the state and headed by someone who himself needed counseling, I would counsel those who came to me.

Knowing that I shouldn't counsel guys alone, my intern from the Remedial Department—who had gone through the same counselor training program at our church that I had—and I decided to team counsel. We set up shop during our free periods wherever there was an unoccupied room.

We were sincerely excited about ministering to the hurts in their lives and leading them in prayers of forgiveness and repentance. We knew that God would heal them and break the cycles of despair in their lives.

"Joyce!" My boss nervously called from the doorway of the library where the intern and I were counseling a student. We had been praying for and with students for about two weeks and had seen amazing results! He slipped inside the room and called again to get my attention.

"Yes?" I replied, trying to keep the irritation out of my voice. *Didn't he see that we were in the middle of serious business for God and shouldn't be interrupted?*

"May I speak with you for a moment?" he persisted. At

that I sighed and went to the door.

"I don't feel good about your doing this, especially on the Center's time," he said softly so as not to be heard by the student. "You'd better stop."

"Stop? When so many guys are getting honest, biblical help?" And to myself I added, *Yeah, the head of counseling would love us to quit; our success is making him look bad!*

"Then we'll do it on our own time. We won't eat lunch, and we'll stay after hours," I brilliantly countered.

He didn't seem happy about this resolution, but having been caught off guard with no protest at hand, he just grimaced, excused himself and left.

Two weeks later I was summoned to the Center director's office. He wasn't happy about the counseling either. Armed to defend myself and the value of the counseling, the discussion became heated.

Finally, in exasperation with me, Sonny bluntly exclaimed, "Do you want to teach here or don't you? We already have a Counseling Department and will have to work within that. It doesn't matter what you think, and it doesn't matter how good your counseling is!"

His voice softened as he continued addressing me earnestly, "Joyce, we don't want to lose you as a teacher. But if you persist in doing what we haven't asked you to do, you'll be out of a job! It's up to you."

In dismay and martyrdom we stopped counseling. But it took only six months to learn the full extent of the damage to my own heart, caused by my critical attitude and presumptuous behavior during those weeks of counseling.

I discovered that when I had acted in presumption—presuming a position I had not been given—coupled with judging others, I opened my heart to other sins. The worst outcome of that counseling experience was that, without the protection of accountability and sensitivity to my authorities, I became deeply connected to the intern! The deep spirit-to-spirit bonding that followed nearly destroyed my family. Although I repented before it became sexual, I had entered a level of worship of human love that broke covenant with God. As I repented during that long, dark winter, the Refiner's fire began burning away the mixed motives in my life.

I learned tremendous lessons at His feet: Don't judge others; do nothing without the approval of my authorities, whether I agree with them or not; and guard my personal spirit. Then God healed me and restored those who had been affected by my arrogance. And in the end, He graciously reestablished His call upon my life.

THE FREQUENT ROUTE OF VISIONARIES

As I look back over the years, I can clearly see the road down which visions and visionaries often travel. The following are signs along that road:

1. God gives us the vision. Passion for it grows in our hearts until it is hard to think of anything else.

91

2. We become frustrated and restless, wondering when God will open the doors and move on our behalf. We begin "helping" Him by promoting ourselves and the vision, pressing hard whenever our authorities or colleagues can't quite seem to get the picture or sense the urgency.

3. We step out on our own, convinced it's the only way to get God's job done. In the process, we judge others and do not seek counsel. We equate the passion in our bones with God's anointing.

4. When the project fails and our zeal is undressed, exposing self-righteousness, we surrender, sometimes in humiliation. The vision essentially dies in our hands, and then we lay it upon the altar. There is sorrow, but God comforts us in the midst of it.

5. As we retreat from others, God begins to reveal the secret, selfish motives that had been in our hearts. We realize that we had taken ownership—and responsibility—for the vision, which we had absolutely no right or ability to maintain. Our impatience is revealed as disbelief that God would keep His word to us.

6. Conviction and repentance take us to our knees.

We surrender our lives again to Him. Now that He has our attention, He begins to apply pressure steadily in every area of our lives in order to instill integrity and character. Intimacy with Him becomes our mainstay. Vision for "great things" is forgotten.

7. Others begin to notice a quiet strength in our lives. They are drawn to us for godly counsel, although we hardly notice, for what we *do* is not a priority anymore.

8. The vision appears again, as though from the dead! We are cautious this time; we make it a matter of great prayer and ponder it in our hearts, saying little to anyone else. If we are to be involved in its coming to pass, we desperately don't want to soil it with fleshly ambition. God alone will have to bring it about, and it must be confirmed by those who know us best.

9. As we sense God moving on our behalf and preparing us in unique ways, we see clearly that His hand has been in it all along. All the stripping and refining were essential preparation for the endurance and maturity level that will be required. We feel very unworthy and inadequate, but we have come to know God and His power.

We know that He can bring it to pass and that He can give us a grace and wisdom not our own to fulfill His plans.

10. Ministry comes forth afresh, this time without fleshly ambition, impatience or pride. Humility has been born, out of which will grow fruit that will remain.[1]

GOD'S ATTENTIVENESS

All of us go through the process of having our motives and character weaknesses exposed. It is not to discourage us, but to cause us to cast ourselves on God and learn His ways in greater depth. It is so that we can get help for our own lives, making us safe to lead others who will look to us to model spiritual and personal health and godliness.

Furthermore, we aren't responsible to make others understand our visions. We aren't responsible to convict others and bring them to their knees when they disagree. Such doings are far beyond what God has asked us to do; if we attempt to do such things, we are truly trying to reign in His place.

However, as we abide in Him daily, embracing the pruning and letting some of our favorite branches be burned in the fire, our fruit grows rich. Eventually it will nourish the world.

ENTRUST THE VISION TO GOD

If we would wait for God to open doors, we would learn our lessons without needless turmoil and too frequent injury. We would also be spared the temptation to become bitter when we don't get our way immediately. It is in the release of our destinies, dying to dreams as *we* might fashion them, that His voice begins to matter, that obedience and holiness take root.

God truly does oppose the proud, and He truly does give grace to the humble (1 Pet. 5:5). So even while the vision burns deep and long within us, we must ask for the other fire—that which refines us by melting to nothing the works of the flesh—the striving, pride and presumption that so easily prey upon visionaries.

We must align ourselves tightly with Him. When we do, we will see that the vision gleams in *His* eye! He is the author of what has taken hold of our hearts. It is His vision. If we attempt to take authorship of it, the best we will be able to produce is a miniature counterfeit, one that will never be able to withstand the heat of high noon labor or the fiery darts of the enemy.

THE PLACE TO GROW

There is a common expression that fits our calling while we wait for the next step to be taken by God. I have never used this expression before because I judged it too simple, but today it must be written: *Bloom where you are planted.*

The beauty of it is that when you bloom, countless seeds are eventually dropped from your life into the soil around you. The blooming *is* important. I have had plants that just endured; they stayed alive just enough to fend off being uprooted and discarded, but they never beautified the landscape or produced more of their kind.

In the quiet, settled place of spirit, even while the world around seems doomed without our being proclaimed its deliverer, the Holy Spirit will begin to speak to us. As self-discipline grows more important—as our time in the Word and prayer increases—the fruit begins to form.

Our sight becomes keener in the waiting. We more often see answers come to simple prayers that were offered behind closed doors, and our faith in God grows. Hope—that assurance that His will truly will triumph—stirs brightly within us, and a spring comes to our step. And love—ah, how easily it is given, and how frequently it comes back to us!

We begin to experience His glory in worship, which drives us in wonder to our knees. That He saved us, that our names are written in the Book of Life, births meekness of the most powerful kind. Time becomes unimportant, and with its passing, we emerge with patience, becoming even-handed and temperate in all our ways.

And our families and friends—even the folks next door—see the change. We don't get angry so easily, and we forgive more quickly. Our longsuffering is a marvel! *But after all,* we muse, *He suffered so long for us. Can we do less for others?*

At this, the flower of our lives opens, and His joy brings us to our feet in praise of Him! How blessed have been our lives! How grateful we are for the very things we had once despised! How could we have doubted His love during the delays?

ON OUR KNEES

To be instruments for His glory will require great discipline of the soul and spirit. That discipline begins when we decide that any seat will do, that we don't need to occupy "first chair" in our section of the orchestra. To *be* in the Symphony is sufficient. To play only as the Maestro directs, presuming nothing but our need to love Him and each other, is enough. His sovereignty is clear and our surrender complete.

GOING DEEPER

1. What stereotypes of women have you let control your responses in life?

2. What is the difference between *presumption* and *assertiveness* in pursuing a ministry goal?

3. Have you known any visionaries who have fallen into sin? What are some of the earmarks of weakness you have observed in them and the way they led others?

4. Name at least three spiritual principles to follow in trying to begin a new ministry within a larger organization.

5. If you feel that God is calling you to begin a completely new, independent ministry, what are five safeguards to ensure the integrity of that ministry?

6. What "branches" do you sense God pruning from your life right now? Are you thanking Him for the pruning, or grumbling over the delay it is causing in pursuing your vision?

7. Have you received confirmation of the vision from people who know you well? Do you have committed prayer intercessors who will stand with you at all times?

Prayer of Commitment for Today:

_____

_____

_____

_____

_____

_____

_____

_____

_____

8

8

Knowing the Score

Am I now trying to win the approval of men, or of God? Or am I trying to please men? If I were still trying to please men, I would not be a servant of Christ.

—GALATIANS 1:10

ong shafts of late afternoon sunlight softly rested on the bookshelves bowed under the ponderous weight of volume after volume of exposition and church history. More books on marriage and counseling filled a bookcase to the left of the door I had entered. On her desk lay various piles of papers and articles she had been perusing before my visit, her Bible open beside them. In the center of it all a computer keyboard stood ready, a half-finished sermon on the computer screen. A picture of her two young children hung on the wall at eye level over the desk.

Janice and her husband, both ordained ministers, co-pastor a growing congregation in Michigan. I had been asking her questions all afternoon about the blessings and difficulties of pastoring. I had one more to ask.

"So, after it is all said and done, what is the hardest part of your calling?" I probed as I watched her face carefully.

She somberly answered with but a hint of a smile about her face and a knowing look in her eyes, "Knowing how to serve people in a way that causes their growth, not their dependency." Then straightening her back she said more emphatically, "Yes, remaining beyond manipulation, doing for them what I discern *God* wants me to do, not what necessarily pleases them or brings me their praise."

Looking at me intently, she continued. "We make a great many mistakes in serving because we are insecure and fear man more than we fear God. While biblical servanthood sounds simple enough, it is vastly opposed to what comes most easily to us in the course of ministering to others. If our serving is out of our own *need to be needed,* strange things can happen."

CONFUSING SLAVING WITH SERVING

When the doorbell rang, everyone at the dinner table groaned. Carolyn, fresh out of seminary and in her first pastorate, glanced up apprehensively.

Leaning back in his chair so that he could see out the side window near the front door, twelve-year-old Robbie spied the visitor.

"Yup. It's Cindy again. Good grief! Doesn't she know it's rude to drop in on folks every night at dinnertime?"

Megan, his senior by three years, nodded disgustedly. "She times it that way to get a free meal! And then Mom has to spend the next two hours up in the bedroom counseling her over some terrible thing that's happened that day. Mom, why does she have to be in crisis every night of the week?" Megan turned to look pleadingly at her mother.

"You just don't understand all the hurts she has had in her life! She needs my help!" Carolyn responded defensively. Then with a touch of frustration in her voice, she quickly added, "I can't stop now; she depends so on me. Please try to understand!"

It was her husband's turn to jump into the fray. "What I understand is that Cindy has taken over our home, abused her welcome and is draining the life out of you! What she needs is to walk out all that you've taught her. Honey, *you're her pastor, not her savior... or her slave!*" With that, Rob slammed down his fork and left the table for the den as Carolyn ran to the door to let Cindy in.

SEEKING APPROVAL

Serving is not simple for men or women. It is a mystery to the human race. Slaving—too many of us understand.

Constantly waiting on someone, subjugating our needs to theirs, is easy at first. We feel that we are ministering sacrificially and nobly. It can actually be self-serving. Our endless charities elicit a measure of approval from the one whom we are accommodating and from those watching. Appeasing them also postpones having to confront them.

But after a while the chains tighten. If we have gained a sense of heightened self-worth from their need of us, we won't know how to stop the slaving even though we are exhausted.

Slaving for others hurts them as well. It never encourages greater responsibility or accountability on their part. They never have to grow up. By slaving we gain only their approval—a very fickle commodity—and they remain takers and slavedrivers as long as we let them.

This happens in Christian service. It happens to pastors, counselors, support staff, youth leaders, musicians, lay care ministers and missionaries. The calling is not really the point: Slaving—serving for approval rather than out of pure obedience and the ultimate maturity of those we serve—will drain the life out of us.

WANTING TO RESCUE

"Can you stay late again tonight to help me work out one last kink in the budget?" Pastor Charles gently urged Sarah from the doorway of her office.

Sarah glanced at her watch, then back at Charles. His big blue eyes won again.

"Sure. I'll come over to your office as soon as I make a quick call home to have Becky start supper for me again. She should be home from cheerleading practice by now."

Her heart began to race a little. She had worked for other pastors before, but never had one of them appreciated her the way Charles did. She really felt special around him. Hopefully Becky would be gracious about her being late again.

"Great!" he beamed as he gave her a wink and a big smile. He left the door ajar and returned to his office down the hall.

By the time she had cleared her desk, made the call and then joined him, all the other staff had gone home. As she entered his office, he jumped up and offered her a chair beside his at his desk. "You're an incredible woman, Sarah. You've raised three kids alone, and you're the best administrator this church has ever had. But best of all, you bring me more joy than you can imagine!"

At that last comment his face clouded, and he added just above a whisper, more to himself than to her, "I wish I could say that about my wife."

That she could mean so much to Charles touched her deeply. How she longed to save him from the heartache he was experiencing in his marriage...

ENSNARED BY FALSE NEED

When we operate in relationships and in ministry out of either inappropriate need or out of the need to be needed, we are sitting ducks for sin. We are in bondage to our own and others' emotional states and vulnerable to manipulators who can see us coming a mile away. There are Carolyns, Sarahs and Charleses strewn all over the Christian ministry landscape. But this does not have to be.

FREED TO PLEASE GOD

Before becoming true servants, we must become freedmen—freed from the power of others' needs, freed to please the Lord alone. Priorities must be restored—worship of God alone and time with Him in which to hear His voice; then care of our families and our own health; and finally, ministering to others. Through it all, we must refuse the lie that we have to prove we are worthy of our callings by burning ourselves out for those who manipulate us by praise or dependency. We must learn that we are no one's savior or slave.

FACT: We will *never* be worthy of our calling, so (blessed relief!) we can stop tearing up our lives and families trying to prove it.

FACT: Servanthood only occurs as we move in step with Jesus. We must do nothing alone: He, the Son of God, the Savior of the world, desires to be in harness with us! Paying attention to Him—not every wave of applause that sweeps the audience nor the temptation to play the savior—will move us and them steadily toward maturity.

FACT: There is a prize to be reached. There is a point to all this "madness" called ministry. It isn't a paycheck, a title or a reputation, and it isn't to feel needed. It is redemption through obedience to God. That is the prize. It is to do only what *He* says to do—what will cause others to see *Him* and grow up—not every grand thing others think we should do.

The disciples—even more so the whole Jewish nation at that time in history—wanted Jesus to do their bidding. They wanted power over their human enemies; they wanted Him to wow the world with His miracles and build a kingdom in which they would be important.

But Jesus kept His eyes on the prize—that salvation would come to you and me, enabling us to embrace the love of God and let the cross break the power of sin and insecurity from our lives. No matter what the enemy—or His friends—wanted Him to do, He held fast to His call. He was a freedman—freed from the temptation of power, position and the praise of man—and therefore freed to serve rather than slave.

POWER UNDER CONTROL

At the heart of servanthood is meekness—one of the greatest mysteries in the world. *Meekness* is power—enormous power—under the control of a higher call than one's own promotion, others' expectations or even our human longings.

Let me illustrate: I have a friend in the ministry whose name is Barbara. She is a beautiful five-foot, four-inch blond, weighs 110 pounds (all in the right places) and has a brilliant mind. She is also very gentle, sensitive and fun-loving, and she attracts admiring men wherever she goes. Barbara could easily exert great control over their lives.

She knows all this. But secure in the knowledge of God's love for herself and for others, she is aware that lordship and saviorhood belong to Jesus alone. She is rightly convinced that her job as a leader is to seek God's perspective first and to respond in such a way that those she leads will sense *God's* presence, not her own. If she discerns the need to speak an unpopular word of truth to that person, she would without fear because of her reverence for God. If silence in the face of an insult is required, she would keep silent rather than defend herself. She knows her value in God, and she knows that He has a plan within the silence to reach the person's heart. On the other hand, when worshipful admiration comes her way, she deflects it to the One who deserves the glory for the good that is in her life.

She knows that no man—no woman—has power over her. She also knows that she cannot exercise power over others because of her respect for God's authority in her life. She answers to a higher call than her own protection or promotion. She is meek. Her power is under control.

HUMILITY

Meekness can never be achieved without humility, seeing ourselves and God accurately. You see, God is God, and *we are not!* Yet God loves us dearly and values us so much that His Son died for us. Our virtues exist only because of what God has become in our lives.

Every day we have opportunities to be great in someone's

eyes and play the savior—sometimes just by letting them love us in ways that they should not.

When we get our roles straight and our eyes fixed on Jesus alone to meet *our* needs, we will be able to act truthfully and confidently for others' good. Then *He* will change their hearts and meet *their* needs.

SERVANTHOOD

Servanthood is a direct result of determining God's perspective on each situation. In order to serve as Jesus would, we must hear from God for ourselves. Then we must act accordingly, even when the action brings no applause and may disappoint some who want us to "perform" for them or "love" them in ways that bring no glory to God. When we focus on doing what shows them the Father's face rather than our own, they will be able to grow up. In the end, if they have been truly seeking God and not simply trying to manipulate or use us selfishly, they will thank us for our obedience.

As we learn to accurately interpret the musical score before us and become free to act in the eternal best interests of others, we will discover true servanthood. It will require keeping our eyes on the prize—the time when the whole world knows Jesus and His cross—so that they too can be qualified to play in the Symphony.

Going Deeper

1. What is your ultimate objective when you serve or help other people who have been hurt or have been in trouble? Have you ever enjoyed their dependency upon you to the point that you are content with their weakness?

2. What are the telltale signs that someone has begun to control you when you have tried to help them?

3. What boundaries must be put in place emotionally and physically when you begin counseling someone? Are you strong enough to enforce them?

4. How can you tell that a person truly desires to change and mature?

5. How can you safeguard yourself against being drained by a leader who expects you to put work or ministry ahead of every other responsibility you have?

6. Are you able to walk away from a ministry worker's flirtatious attention?

7. Describe Christ's example of servanthood to His disciples and to the women who followed Him.

Prayer of Commitment for Today:

_____

_____

_____

_____

_____

_____

_____

_____

_____

_____

9

Reaching a New Level of Skill

I do not consider myself yet to have taken hold of it. But one thing I do: Forgetting what is behind and straining toward what is ahead, I press on toward the goal to win the prize for which God has called me heavenward in Christ Jesus.

—PHILIPPIANS 3:13–14

Failure in leadership can be caused by divisive, stubborn followers–or because of hidden sin in the ranks, as in the case of Joshua's defeat at Ai. Beyond those reasons, traditionally when *male* leaders have failed, it seems most often to have been because of insensitivity, autocratic methods or inability to grasp and convey vision for the ministry. On the other hand, when *female* leaders have failed, it has been most often because of a lack of both emotional boundaries and commitment to disciplining their natural tendencies.

In the first place, we women have complex reactions to situations and have had little training in how to clearly define that for which we are really responsible. As a result, we can easily become emotionally drained and psychologically exhausted, then carry the load home with us. In the second place, we allow stereotypical behavior to go unchallenged in our lives. As a result, we receive stereotypical treatment by others, especially men. Even worse, we become mired in the present, neglecting the pursuit of personal growth and development.

ASSUMING UNDUE RESPONSIBILITY

Entering the classroom that morning, I knew something was amiss.

"Tony's gone, Sister Strong. He left last night. After taking a swing at his roommate and cursing up a storm, he just packed his duffel bag and walked away!" John, one of my student teachers, whispered to me as I hung up my coat on the hook beside my office door.

I was stunned. I had worked with Tony personally for several months when he had first come into Teen Challenge as a remedial student. Even after turning him over to an assistant, I had kept in close touch with his progress and had talked with him often. Everyone was rooting for his success—especially me. He had seemed happy and upbeat about everything! What had gone wrong?

"Did someone provoke him?" I asked suspiciously. John

shook his head no. And then remembering Tony's probationary status with the Center, I anxiously asked, "Do the police know he's gone yet?"

Before he could reply, I knew the answer. Of course, they did. By law we had to alert them the minute anyone probated by the courts to us left the grounds.

But a bigger question was pressing in on me. Why hadn't I known that he was struggling? What kind of a teacher am I anyway that I don't pick up on such monumental issues before something like this happens? I commenced to tear myself up with blame—and fear for Tony.

I stumbled through the day, but just before going home I purposely stopped by Sonny's office. As I called his name through the three inches his door was ajar, he stopped what he was doing and invited me in.

As I sat in dejection on the edge of the chair he'd offered me, I got right to the point. "Tony left last night."

"Yes, he did," Sonny replied seriously.

"Why didn't I realize he was struggling with something and help him? I wasn't there for him at all!" I started to cry.

Sonny cleared his throat and looked at me squarely. "Joyce, did you do the best you could during the months you were working with him?" he asked quietly.

I thought a minute. "Yes, I think I did. I had no idea he was angry or frustrated."

"And does Tony have a free will?" Sonny continued persistently.

"Of course!"

"And can you change anyone's free will?" was the next question Sonny put to me.

Before I could answer, he said, "Tony had it in his heart to leave. It was something he had intentionally hidden from everyone. No one could have made him do other than what he wanted to do. Neither you nor anyone else but Tony determined his choice."

The next question choked me up and has never left me. "Do you think you are God?" he asked gently. "Could you have saved Tony? Can you save anyone for that matter? Joyce, you did the best you knew to do in dealing with him, and God is pleased with that."

He paused a moment, and then, repositioning himself in his chair, he pressed on. "I don't want you ever to stop caring about the students, but you must learn to allow others to be who they are and not carry the burden of their choices. If you don't learn this, you will simply get in the way, and your emotions will confuse the issue every time," he asserted firmly but kindly. "God loves Tony more than you or I do, and He can deal with Tony's choices. Perhaps prison time is the only thing that will cause Tony to take his relationship with God seriously."

I had not thought of that! I had been reacting out of my relationship with Tony and my false assumption that I should be able to solve all his problems. I had lost sight of the bigger picture and, more specifically, the love and sovereignty of God.

"Joyce, you're a good teacher. But if you let your emotions play into every situation, you will not be able to hear from

116

God. Your greatest responsibility is to live in obedience to God in your own life, keeping Him on the throne. Deal with issues from a position of integrity day by day to the best of your ability. As you are responsible for your own choices, God will hold others responsible for theirs."

Sonny leaned forward on his elbows and continued. "You are not God. You are not omniscient nor can you save anyone else. There are some things for which you are simply not responsible. If you carry everyone else's reactions into your own emotions, you'll go crazy! That's not your job!"

Finally he smiled. "Just go do what you were hired to do. Be sensitive, but keep your emotions free. Don't be a slave to them. God will take care of others' choices." The room grew silent as I sat there just letting it all sink in.

"One more thing," he finally added. "Let's pray and release Tony to the Lord. Then go home and have some fun with your family!" Sonny grinned like a kid.

We prayed. And as I left in my car a few minutes later, I burst into song. In fact, I sang at the top of my lungs all the way home.

Learning to Think Objectively

I deeply appreciated the wisdom Sonny shared with me that day. I also am indebted to other effective leaders who have demonstrated how to put personal sentiment aside when a problem must be confronted in another person. When this is done, issues can be honestly and objectively

117

addressed without fear or emotional bias. I have seen my husband deal calmly with a very sticky situation at work, even one in which he could perceive himself as being attacked, and still be friends with the person the next day. *The point is to separate the problem from the words and moods, dissecting it and then resolving it one simple step at a time.*

When we learn to focus on the problem instead of the person, we will also be much less apt to say something we'll regret later. Even if the discussion becomes heated, we won't take personal swipes at the other person. Once the problem is solved, the tension will end.

Most men have a natural tendency to be problem solvers, and many women need to learn from them. Men love tackling a dilemma and coming up with an answer. The problem is less likely to become a personal issue to a man—but can easily become personal to a woman. Women are more relational in orientation.

But women, we can *learn* to think more linearly, one issue at a time. We can become effective problem solvers as we discipline our minds to sort out the facts from the feelings and align the facts with a step-by-step resolution. We *can* go home from a hectic day and forget about it—and oh, how our families will love that! We can *discipline* ourselves to tackle the issue first. When the issue is resolved, God may want us to help the person grow emotionally, but that's another story.

OUR OWN GROWTH IS POSSIBLE

Through the years of working predominantly alongside men, I have seen many qualities of leadership that I have asked God to work into my own life. I do not believe that men only can have these qualities of leadership. Generalities such as saying "That's a man thing" or "That's a woman thing" have stymied much growth that could be taking place in both sexes. Failing to resist being stereotyped can prevent us from breaking out of traditional, stereotypical patterns into new growth and self-discipline.

The Power of Stereotypes

One stereotype we have taken to our hearts without resistance is the notion that women must talk a great deal. It seems to be general knowledge that women utter about three times as many words in a day as do men. This understanding is based on observation—but is it a *necessity?* Or is it just what is expected, therefore unresisted by us?

This reminds me of a conversation I overheard in the grocery store between the mothers of teenage boys:

"Well, you know how it is with teenagers. You can't count on them for anything! What's the use of expecting them to be helpful around the house? They'll never do it!" exclaimed one mom.

"I know just what you mean!" the second mom chimes in.

"I *never* know where Jon is at night, so why bother to ask him to be home?"

"Well, kids'll be kids, I guess," the first mom rejoins. "Just wait 'til they're parents! Then they'll get theirs!"

At this both moms break out laughing. As they steer their shopping carts away, they shake their heads and plod on.

BREAKING FREE OF EXPECTATIONS

The conversation between those mothers distressed me. All I knew was that our teenage son was thoughtful, and we always knew where he was. If he was going to be late, he called and explained, setting our minds at ease. I had to wonder if many teenagers simply acted out the path of least resistance because their parents expected no better of them and invested little time in teaching them to do otherwise.

This led me to consider the stereotypes that circulate about women. For instance, even though millions of jokes have been told about how women talk incessantly, *must* we *say* everything that is on our minds? Are we not also sometimes simply taking the path of least resistance? Is it possible to develop a more reflective mind-set?

While I do tend to process situations and decisions verbally more often than mentally, I have been challenging myself to listen more and talk less. It takes discipline, but I am learning to process my feelings and thoughts more thoroughly before speaking.

As God places me in more areas of leadership, I am

increasingly aware of the importance of holding my tongue until I have all the information. Amazingly, I can do it! I believe that it is an important step in disciplining myself to hear more easily from God, as well as to be more sensitive to those around me—particularly men.

Our Need to Listen

As we work side by side with men in ministry—just as in marriage—we can wear them out with excessive verbiage! In the natural, it can be our greatest weapon of intimidation, but at the same time it always gives them a perfect way to get even—by not listening! But engaging in a war is not our goal in ministry or marriage, so let's learn to use our words sparingly and with as much meaning as possible.

Learn to really *listen* to what others have to say, whether they are right or wrong—to follow their train of thought and hear their hearts, which we are gifted at doing if we give ourselves a chance. When being challenged, let's not listen just long enough to gather ammunition for our next barrage of words. Incidentally, if we become sincere listeners, the chances will greatly increase that men will take the initiative in communicating with us about something other than the weather!

Whether they realize it or not, men also have a great need in the area of communication—to discipline themselves to be more expressive, more trusting with their words. We can hear from God more clearly by talking less and listening more; men can draw near to God more intimately by

121

learning to express the wealth that is in their hearts.

We both need to stretch to embrace each other's strengths in these areas. It can be done!

Men need not be limited to projecting an image of "the strong, silent type" or the heartless "macho man." Nor are we doomed to being the "dumb blonde" or the "nagging shrew." Together we are the dwelling place of God. We are joint heirs with Christ, kings and priests in the service of Almighty God!

Meanwhile, we should value the special qualities that God has lovingly shaped within us as women, qualities that are greatly needed, particularly in leadership roles within the ministry. The most outstanding and universal ones are:

- Intuitiveness in determining a person's character

- Instinct for sensing danger in a decision

- Ability to work well in teams to accomplish a common goal

- Sensitivity to those under our authority

- Willingness to hear many opinions and arrive at consensus without feeling threatened as a leader

- Ability to work tirelessly for a godly cause

- Comparative ease in pursuing intimacy with God

GOD'S PLAN

With precision God uses the sculptor's hammer to refine each character quality in our lives. Just as a great artist gives complete attention to detail, He moves in rhythm with us through every turn of events in our lives, shaping and molding us into useful vessels.

Meanwhile, God will place men and women in our lives who have walked this way ahead of us. They understand the breaking and shaping work of God and will be able to encourage us and help us get the most out of the lessons.

I have yet to meet anyone more fulfilled than a woman who has successfully come through the fire and out from under the sculptor's tools aimed at the old nature within. For us as well, life *gains* rather than *loses* meaning as we relinquish our supposed power as independent women, captains of our fates, masters of our souls. In dying to ourselves in the midst of adversity—refusing to curse but only bless—the very power that raised Christ from the dead moves into our lives!

As His character grows within us, others will begin asking us to lead them! Our giftings and yieldedness to the Holy Spirit will qualify us. With His life and power within, effective ministry is finally possible.

CRISIS PRECEDED USEFULNESS

It is very valuable to be aware of where we are in the stages of

personal and spiritual growth. If we are in a particularly difficult stage, it is encouraging to know that it will not last forever!
On the other hand, if we are in a rich place of deep service to
others, seeing where God has taken us and where we are going
increases our gratitude and prepares us for the next adventure.

As we reflect upon the seasons of our lives we will note that
*crisis always precedes great usefulness and increased aware-
ness of God.* The Refiner's fire burns away our selfish, wrong
motives. His hammer breaks us free from all bondage, and
His love pulls us to Himself through it all.

In my case, when I asked God to burn out of my life anything that could come between Him and me, His flame
torched "my ministry," my spiritual pride, my hunger for
approval and my fear of man. I finally faced and dealt with
problems that had been repressed for most of my life.

I was driven to the Rock—to complete dependence upon
God for the first time in my life. God faithfully worked a miracle in my heart and circumstances that gave birth to a rich
future. Many tears were shed in the flames, and cries truly did
rise when the hammer fell, but with all my heart I am grateful
beyond words for His love in bringing growth to my life.

The truth about us is revealed in a crisis. If we pay close
attention during the turmoil, it will teach us valuable lessons
about how to deal with conflict within ourselves and with
others in the future. It is a time when God stretches our per-
spectives by revealing the narrowness of the ones by which
we had been living. Through the death to self that emerges,
God will actually enlarge our capacity to minister to others.

And all the while He will cradle us and pour His tenderness into our hearts as we repent or forgive—whichever is needed to assuage the fire and the hammer. Slowly the compassion that will enable us to suffer for the sake of Christ is born.

MATURITY GAINED

Our lives finally find their resting place in Him, and we know who we are! A quietness descends upon the way we deal with issues as we listen for His voice before we speak. We have learned to process events through His eyes and have developed great self-control when under pressure.

Our lives have been tuned like fine instruments by the Maestro who meets us in solitude, and we play for Him alone. And as the song that has begun in our spirits spills out in selfless service, we bow in awe before the Composer who could pen such grace!

NEW HOPE

And then appears the promise: Someday we will not play alone. Our pulses quicken at the thought that there might be others who, like us, are discovering the secret of the Symphony.

This season of separation will pass. Someday we will be together—after the fire, the hammer and the solitude have brought us to a greater level of musical skill, prepared to play for *His* glory alone.

Going Deeper

1. What are a woman's unique strengths—spiritually, mentally, emotionally and physically? How can these strengths benefit her in ministry?

2. Can any of these qualities work against you when under stress? If so, how?

3. How do you determine when you have reached the end of your influence for good on someone's life and must give him or her to God?

4. How effective are you at separating your emotions from the facts in solving interpersonal problems? Try to describe how you address such problems.

5. What feminine stereotype(s) would you like to break in your own life?

6. Describe, if you can, a situation in which you were a good listener when working with a man. How did your attentiveness affect, if at all, his willingness to trust your judgment or opinion?

7. What qualities do you see in godly male leaders around you that you would like God to develop within you?

❧

Prayer of Commitment for Today:

_____

_____

_____

_____

_____

_____

_____

_____

_____

_____

10

❦

The Support of
Other Musicians

*For you know that we dealt with each of you as a
father deals with his own children, encouraging,
comforting and urging you to live lives worthy of
God, who calls you into his kingdom and glory.*

—1 THESSALONIANS 2:11

Nikki Kull, vice president for residential programs at the
New Mexico Boys and Girls Ranches in Albuquerque,
New Mexico, asked the group a simple question: "What are
some of the problems you deal with among your staff?"
Hands shot up, and answers were readily volunteered:

- Control
- Anger
- Victim mentality
- Egos in conflict

129

- Racial tension
- Age discrimination
- Power
- Jealousy
- Lack of productivity
- No accountability

The setting for this discussion was a workshop titled "Confronting Problem Behavior in the Church and Other Ministries" at the National Church Business Administrators Convention held in Breckinridge, Colorado.

Yes, in churches we face the same flesh faced in the secular workplace—and unfortunately we often know less about how to handle the problems that ensue than the world does.

SOLVING OUR PROBLEMS

Several years ago when Teen Challenge wanted a seminar on workplace issues, we had to enlist the services of a secular organization to teach us! I was amazed at the wisdom they brought to us. It seemed that the world had discovered many of *our* principles—though they left out the Word—principles we had not disciplined ourselves to teach and use preventively in our own ministry.

Today, thank God, there are slowly emerging teams of Christian men (and sometimes women) who are offering similar seminars based on God's Word. We are realizing that what is "spiritual" can also be practical and needs to be approached as such and implemented. We must catch up with the world in taking care of our own.

AN ADMONITION

Are we personally susceptible to such weaknesses and sins as were listed in Nikki's workshop session? Are there patterns of the flesh we have unwittingly carried with us into our "new life in Christ"? Is there a battle yet to be won in our lives? How best can we be held accountable for the renewing of our minds and the taking on of the character of Christ—which is our ultimate goal?

The strain on women in all areas of work and ministry is great. In order to ensure our place—especially in leadership—and command the respect of others, we get the feeling that we must be even better at what we do than our male counterparts.

While it is a trap to think that we must earn our way through striving for perfection, there is a well-taken admonition within this dilemma: We need to be healthy emotionally and secure spiritually, trained scripturally in character and held accountable for our lives and ministries.

UNIVERSAL NEED FOR HEALING

Christians come from diverse backgrounds. I was raised in a protective Christian home where I accepted Jesus as my savior at an early age. I loved the Lord with all my heart, yet as an adult, I found myself striving for approval, afraid of failure and stuffing hurts because I thought that Christians were supposed to endure hardship like good soldiers, confusing sin with persecution for Christ's sake.

On the other hand, I know a young woman who has been saved only a few years, raised by a mother who continually had affairs and a father who was an alcoholic. Meg has struggled to believe in God's faithfulness and unconditional love for her, feeling unworthy and rejected.

The point is that both of us have needed and have taken advantage of personal Christian counseling to sort out the issues in our lives. Through it, God has exposed controlling thought patterns for what they are: lies that Satan uses to keep us in defeat.

HELP IN THE BODY

Thank God for Christians in the body of Christ who are gifted in discernment, mercy and exhortation and who are called to come alongside others and lead them to the Lord for emotional and spiritual healing. They give us the opportunity to express what we don't dare tell anyone else—the things that will expose the lies we have believed about ourselves, others and God. They can show us the truth from the Word and encourage us to receive God's provision for all our difficulties. They can help us see where repentance and forgiveness are necessary and assist us in praying for the breaking of strongholds in our lives, bringing us lasting deliverance.

DISCIPLING

From there, after the rotten roots in our lives have been

destroyed and healing received by the power of the Holy Spirit, we can be discipled in the truth. The battle, as Neil Anderson, author of *The Bondage Breaker,* says, is for our minds, so the assimilation of God's Word is critical. It is the truth that sets us free and keeps us free. We must be taught how to take every thought captive and how to renew our minds through "the washing with water through the word," as the apostle Paul encouraged us to do (Eph. 5:26). We will not live in victory without the Word instilled in us.

Discipling can occur in a small group that meets regularly to study God's Word or in a relationship found with a mature believer for that purpose. Bible school can provide discipling experiences as long as there is an accounting for our faith and belief in what we are learning.

MENTORING

Mentoring is like discipling in that it is centered around the Word. But while discipling is geared more to mastering the facts and inferences of the Word and coming to faith in them, the goal of mentoring is to show us by example how to apply scriptural principles to our everyday lives.

A *mentor* is someone who has excelled in the lifestyle or area of professional endeavor we are pursuing and offers us a model—a tutor—one who holds us accountable to apply what we are learning. I am blessed to be able to learn from the life and wisdom of Mara Crabtree, a professor at Regent University. She is a soft-spoken woman of deep integrity and love for women in ministry, a delightful lady who knows who she is in God. The quality of the contribution she is making to the education of women in a male-dominated setting has earned her great respect among her peers as well as the students.

Mara has a tremendous gift for asking the right questions to guide me in seeing for myself God's answer for any struggle I am having. Her prophetic insight and discerning prayers have also encouraged me many times. I, in turn, mentor younger women who are coming along behind me as I am behind Mara.

WE NEED HELP

Especially as women, we need to seek out and enlist mentors in the ministry. Men have been mentoring one another in ministry for centuries, so we have a lot of catching up to do! It may be difficult to find other women to mentor us, particularly in leadership positions, but to do so will prove invaluable.

Hopefully in the years ahead Christian organizations will spring up all over the country to provide mentoring connections for women in ministry. I know of a few Christian universities that have such organizations, but we need many more to handle the demand that is now here. We need easily accessible places to receive counsel regarding matters unique to women in any form of ministry—prayer support, referral services for women who are retreat and conference speakers, mentoring connections and periodic seminars on subjects relevant to Christian women in leadership in ministry and the marketplace.

Someday I believe organizations like this will have an impact on women all across the country. For now, however, if we have no such organization in our area and there are no women available who are seasoned in the ministry to which God is calling us, we can ask our pastors to recommend mature couples whom they know well who would be willing to take us on.

In carefully structured situations men could mentor us, but it would of necessity have to be purely job-related instruction, to avoid the danger of "connecting." Discussion of personal issues should be with another woman, not a man.

PRINTED RESOURCES

In addition to mentoring, there is a vast wealth of leadership and ministry-related teaching in print, especially in periodicals such as *Leadership Journal* and *Ministries Today*. Most of it is geared to men and written by men, but we can glean a great deal from these sources. And as we women grow, we must write for others what we have learned. A newer magazine, *SpiritLed Woman,* has begun with just such a focus in mind.

MATURITY

Each of these—counselor, discipler and mentor—can be of

tremendous help in bringing about our maturity. Their purpose is never to be a replacement for the Holy Spirit and our own personal pursuit of God, but to keep us facing the Father's love, appropriating the completed work of Christ on the cross and walking in obedience through the power of His resurrection.

No person is to control or govern our lives. God is our final authority, and we can hear from Him for ourselves. They are not to be our crutches or our decisionmakers, nor are they to be viewed in any way as our saviors.

Their involvement in our lives is usually only for a season—a given period of time with a given goal in mind. But there should always be *someone* in our lives whom we have asked to hold us accountable, especially as we minister to others. This person must be of trustworthy character, personal integrity and able to keep confidence.

ACCOUNTABILITY

My husband and I are in a special relationship with one other couple for the purpose of mutual accountability and support. We pray for each other and give input when asked regarding major decisions. We are there for each other in a crisis and cheer each other on in our respective ministries.

There is great safety in being known well by those whom we trust to tell us the truth. It is when we move into isolation from others' insights that we can become self-deluded or deceived. There is safety in remaining forever vulnerable to counsel and correction. The enemy can bushwhack us from our blind side when we travel alone. Especially in the ministry we need eyes in the backs of our heads—and the mature believers around us in concert with the Holy Spirit can be those eyes for us.

OUR UNIQUE NEEDS

This morning I stopped on impulse at a landscape nursery I had never visited before. Many times I had driven by and peered curiously down the long lane trying to size up the enterprise. But I sensed today was the day for a "divine encounter," as I parked my car and headed for the salesroom.

There I met the owners—two women probably in their late thirties or early forties—who have obviously labored hard and long to make this business a success. The environment they have created is like a massive garden, artistically laid out and stretching to press against its surrounding border of native woods. It is more a park than a yard of stock for sale.

Somehow we got on the subject of women and the obstacles they have to overcome in this life. One woman, weathered and strong with a no-nonsense air about her, surprised me by expressing very readily the difference as she saw it between that with which women and men wrestle in this life.

As she stood behind the counter—her work-worn hands bagging my peat moss—she said with a degree of intensity in her voice, "What men struggle with comes mostly from outside themselves—the stuff they do to themselves. We have not only that struggle—but we also struggle with stuff inside. For forty years we have a monthly cycle that puts us through changes emotionally and physically; we have to bear and raise children, and we enter into relationships with others that are often very hard on us. And we just have to keep on going."

Looking me in the eye, she added with finality, "Women are much stronger than men realize."

I thought a lot about her words as I continued the trip home and unloaded the shrub I had bought. We are sometimes like giant shock absorbers bearing the jostling and weight of everyone around us!

OUR NEED FOR A "BUDDY"

That realization caused me to be impressed all the more with our need to receive help from others more mature in the faith and to have a buddy, a confidante, a friend with whom we can laugh and cry and pray. Such a friend doesn't have to have all the answers; she doesn't have to be "spiritual" all the time, but she must be someone who is safe to unload on about the everyday frustrations so that we can breathe again. And we must be there for her as well!

This buddy is someone with whom we can goof off, talk heavy stuff just to explore ideas, someone for whom we don't have to "fix our faces." This friend keeps us laughing but isn't put off by our tears. In fact, when we cry, she cries! She helps us not to take ourselves too seriously; with her we can expose our most stupid moments and laugh about them for an hour if we need to! She helps us get hold of the "big picture" by letting us dump out the trivia that may have overwhelmed us.

IN SPITE OF DISTANCE

My best buddy lives in Florida. Since we moved to North Carolina it has been very hard to stay close, but we manage. We call each other whenever we hurt or just want to talk or share some great news about our kids. We ask each other's advice, but we don't have to be Miss Answer Lady for each other. We just need to be ourselves.

She was the first person other than my parents who told me that she would love me no matter what I did. (In fact, I don't remember my parents telling me that, although they have proven they would.) God sent her into my life when my marriage was being turned inside out and all its messy seams were being exposed, and I didn't know if my husband and I were going to make it. I desperately needed to hear a human being tell me what Jesus wanted me to know as well: "I'll love you no matter what."

She let me know that I needed to do good things for myself sometimes. And I remember that fact now when I've been pushing to meet project deadlines or preparing for days for speaking at a retreat or seminar. I then schedule a day at the beach or lunch with one of the new friends God has given me in Raleigh. Her encouragement reminds me how I need to take walks in the woods that I love so much and that echo God's own love and kindness! In fact, I see Him most clearly on those days when I am not demanding anything profound of myself, just as she didn't, even though I "feel His pleasure" when I am doing my best for His glory.

TAKING CARE OF OURSELVES

For many of us it is easier to pay attention to our spiritual and emotional health than it is to take care of our bodies! But we must be healthy and self-disciplined to stay that way out of respect for the lives God has given us. Furthermore, we are His dwelling place and His ambassadors to the world. We want to be at our best so that we will have the strength and energy to follow where He leads.

We must never get too busy with "ministry" to take care of our bodies. We need to exercise regularly, even if it is just a twenty-minute brisk walk each day, preferably in a peaceful, natural environment. Not only will we feel refreshed and rejuvenated physically, but we will find that our lives come back into perspective as we experience the "great outdoors." Such times provide solitude, unstructured worship and reflection on God's love for us.

Also, we must eat sensibly and control our weight. If we find ourselves consistently using food as a reward for success or for solace when we are discouraged, we have let it take God's place in our lives. Calling our mentor, counselor or buddy at such a time to pray with us and direct our emotions and hearts to God *before* we escape into food will hold us accountable and get us beyond the temptation.

If we neglect ourselves and continue to "stuff" the things that steal our sleep and drive us to discouragement, we will never be able to play a right note in the Symphony to come. The issues that threaten to disable us must be faced. They are nothing of which to be ashamed; they only call out to be resolved.

WHEN WE ARE READY

We are His precious musicians. We are the ones with whom He intends to play His music with exquisite precision when we are ready. It is wise to embrace the support of other musicians who love the Maestro as we do. Through them He will heal whatever is broken inside so the music can flow as it should. Someday we will hear, "Well done!" as the curtain falls for the last time.

Going Deeper

1. Are there any areas of your personal life for which you feel you need inner healing counseling? Have you made the need known to anyone who could guide you to a Christian professional or trained lay counselor?

2. Do you belong to a small group that studies the Bible and actively applies its principles to life? If not, what are your plans for joining one or finding a strong believer who is willing to disciple you personally?

3. Who in the body of Christ has already successfully walked the ministry path that you believe God is calling you to walk? Write or call that person, telling her about yourself and your vision, asking her to consider spending time with you periodically so that you can learn from her and her experience.

4. Whom have you asked to hold you accountable to live a responsible and godly life right where you are? Are you completely honest with that person? What may happen down the road if you are not honest now?

5. Who is your "buddy"? If you do not have one, what has hindered you from having such a relationship?

6. What are some of the difficulties in having close friends as a leader in ministry? What is the value of networking with women leaders from ministries other than your own for friendship?

Prayer of Commitment for Today:

11

*When Playing
by Heart*

Above all else, guard your heart, for it is the well-spring of life.

—PROVERBS 4:23

I have left the most serious topic for last—the most pervasive blight in the ministry, but the least often discussed.

Remember Sarah and Pastor Charles from chapter eight? She is an administrator in his church, and he has persuaded her again to stay late and work on the budget with him. As usual, the rest of the staff have gone home, and they are alone in the building.

THE SETUP

As Sarah settled into the comfortable leather chair that Charles had placed alongside his behind the large, oak desk in his office, her arm accidentally bumped lightly against his. Charles turned and looked at her warmly, with surprise on his face.

"Why, even when you bump against me, you're gentle!" he laughed. "And you're pretty, too. Did I ever tell you how refreshing it is to see your lovely face each morning?" Not waiting for a reply he continued, "It makes coming to work an absolute pleasure!" His voice was deep and smooth, with a slight hint of intimacy growing in it.

To be this close to a man again—and such a handsome one at that—after ten years of divorced singleness is intoxicating, Sarah reflected silently, drawing a deep breath.

As he sorted out the sheaves of paper on his desk looking for the budget balance sheet, she began to really notice his hands—large, but not clumsy, nails neatly trimmed, with a wide wedding band on his left hand.

His wife! The words came to Sarah with a jolt. Suddenly she was aware of the small picture of Linda that stood on the credenza behind them.

"Charles, I feel as if your wife is watching us," Sarah said with a nervous laugh. At his puzzled look, she pointed over his left shoulder to the picture.

"Oh, that's no problem," he smiled with resolve and promptly swung around in his chair and laid Linda's picture

146

face down. "Not that we're doing anything she shouldn't see, but just to make you more comfortable," he added with that twinkle in his eye again.

No, we're not doing anything wrong, Sarah thought to herself. *We have to sit together to go over the budget, and I can't help it if I bumped him. Furthermore, what's wrong with finally being appreciated for being pretty? Besides, I'm a big girl, and he's a man of God!*

At that Sarah refocused on the matter at hand with renewed confidence. She fleetingly wondered if it had been such a good idea to wear this low-necked sundress today—his gaze seemed to be dropping to her neckline a bit often!

Well, so what! she told herself. *If you've got it, flaunt it!*

That last thought caught her by surprise. Had she really said that to herself? Where'd that come from?

Right at that moment his hand gently brushed hers to get her attention. It got her attention—not to see the paperwork on his desk, but to look into those captivating blue eyes of his. They now had a hunger in them, a longing for her that fairly took her breath away!

Could this wonderful, tender godly man actually want her? Did she really, as he had many times said, have qualities long missing in his wife?

How could any woman not give this man all he wanted? He was nothing but kindness!

The touch had baited her. Now the longing for intimacy with this man welled up and overflowed her heart. Surely it showed in her eyes.

Yes, he saw it, and he made the move he had fantasized about for over a year now. He quickly stood and pushed his chair aside. Bending over her, he gently drew her out of her chair and into his arms.

Just one kiss, he told himself. *That will be enough.*

But it wasn't enough, and the song of hell began. All the late nights, lunches out together under the pretext of working, the "chance meetings" in the park, the long talks about their heartaches and dreams had set the stage well for this event.

As their emotions surged, their spirits were ripped apart by this deadly betrayal.

BACK TO THE BEGINNING

So whose fault *is* sexual sin in the ministry? Could the Garden of Eden experience teach us something valuable? Is the root of all sin lodged in Adam's choosing Eve over God in the Garden? Did he neglect *true* love for the moment—love that would deny himself her approval and say, "No, I won't eat that thing with you or we'll both die!"? Or did Eve use her feminine wiles to entice him to eat rather than obey God?

WHO'S RESPONSIBLE?

As I searched my own rearing in the church to find some answers to my questions, I remembered the "Christian" book I had been given by my mother when I was a teenager. It explained the "facts of life" and set guidelines for propriety in dating. The overriding impression I was left with was that sexual purity was up to me; the guy could not be held responsible because his sex drive was so strong! Therefore, I must be the one to draw the line. I must wear conservative clothing so as not to provoke him, and I must say *no* to his advances because he cannot.

Even as a naïve fourteen-year-old, something about this didn't seem right. Such a philosophy seemed to me to debase both of us. As the responsibility was put upon me and the guy was excused, I felt defeated before I began.

OUR RELIGIOUS LEGACY

The Pharisees—our religious forefathers—did much to influence what the church unwittingly believes, as reflected in the book I read as a teenager. While the religious Jews accommodated men's abdication of self-control (by multiple wives and the ability to divorce at will), women were reduced to the image of temptress—the man's downfall. These men established a power base domestically and religiously upon the assertion that Eve was to blame for the Fall—the same excuse that Adam made to God for his own lack of self-control and disobedience in the Garden. Therefore, religious Jews kept women in seclusion, uneducated and subservient on the premise that this would reduce sin among the men.

PERSISTENT SCAPEGOAT MENTALITY

Today when I see women covered in great swaths of cloth on a 100-degree day at Disney World while their husbands sport T-shirts, shorts and sandals, I am reminded of this philosophy. Their dress and the fact that they must walk behind the men graphically demonstrate the scapegoat mentality perpetuated by religious Jewish leaders: It is women's beauty that brings sin; therefore, it must be reduced and hidden. The women pay the price for both Adam and Eve as though Adam had been powerless to resist. By their dress and subservience the bundled women symbolically carry the guilt of them both!

Abortion does this as well. The woman is still taking responsibility for an act that she did not perform alone. While the man who impregnated her moves on unrestrained, she "chooses" not only the elimination of a member of the next generation, but also any reminder of the man's guilt and responsibility before society.

EQUAL RESPONSIBILITY

Jesus hit the issue head on. He set Jewish men back on their heels by telling them that even to lust—to play those games of sexual conquest in their minds—was as dangerous as doing the act, and it must stop. Whether in their minds or in their flesh, lust would destroy intimacy with God and violate the object of the lust. This was a call to self-control, sexual responsibility and commitment to God and women that the men had not had to deal with before!

Jesus was also very pointed when He spoke—however forgivingly—to the woman caught in adultery. He said that she must not continue sinning—that the seductive patterns of her life must be stopped. *She too had to learn self-control and sexual responsibility if she were to follow Him and avoid spiritual death.*

The apostle Paul as well knew the patterns of the world and the enemy, and he had his hands full dealing with all kinds of new Christians! He offered guidelines to *both the men and the women* on this subject of shared responsibility for matters of the heart.

MEN HELD ACCOUNTABLE

After centuries of being able to have several wives and divorce at will, Paul laid down a very new edict for the men in 1 Timothy 3:1–5: To be an elder in the Christian church, a man must be sexually responsible and have only one wife. (He did not have to give this command to women because they had never been allowed to practice polygamy.) A man must also have his house in order, which meant he would have to be deeply and permanently involved with his family. Furthermore, he must be self-controlled in matters of temper, disposition and money. No more could he be a law unto himself.

Paul also told men to deny themselves and in love to lay

down their lives for their wives so that their wives would not be defiled. They were to love unselfishly their wives in the same way Jesus loved His precious church (Eph. 5:25–30)! This was an amazing turn of events for the cultures of that day—Jewish, Greek and Roman! He went on to say that the man will leave his family for *her*—throughout Jewish history, the woman had left her family for him (Eph. 5:31)! Furthermore, in 1 Peter 3:7, Paul warns that inconsideration of his wife will hinder a man's own prayers!

Women Held Accountable

Regarding the women newly converted from the cult of Diana, a group of women accustomed to leading by seduction and prostitution, Paul gave warning not to allow them positions of authority. It was to prevent them from dominating or controlling men through the use of their femininity, as they were used to doing. They must first learn from others in full yieldedness to their teachers (1 Tim. 2:11–12). (Paul had no problem with women teachers who were learned and mature, such as Priscilla, whom he commended. Paul's overarching concern was always unity and the maturity of all in the body of Christ.)

Paul also told the Ephesian women in 1 Timothy 2:9–10 to pay attention to the way they presented themselves in appearance. They were to understand that the good deeds that came out of their hearts were what made them beautiful, not all the fancy stuff they used to put on. They were to be modest—not drawing attention to their sexuality—and take responsibility to reflect the new life within them.

MUTUAL RESPECT

The message from Jesus and from Paul is that men and women were responsible to get real and do something about their sinful pasts, weaknesses and selfish patterns of behavior toward each other. *Then,* they could minister in His name.

Yes, they were to be one another's keeper. In fact, if anyone sinned against one of God's little ones, it would be better for him or her to be drowned with a millstone around his or her neck (Matt. 18:6). How much plainer could Jesus make it that they must not sin against each other, but rather esteem each other highly in unselfish love? Today, two thousand years later, the same message can bring new life to the church.

THE CURE

There is no amount of governmental legislation that will restore our value, teach men to be responsible and bring sanity back to our culture outside or inside the church. Only the repentance of men for devaluing us—rather than honoring us as equally made in God's image—and our repentance for looking to men's love to save us or give us viability—and sometimes enticing them in hopes of getting that love—will start the healing process. As more of us are being called by God and qualified to minister in the body of

Christ alongside men, we must get our acts together. Our hearts—and minds—must be changed.

Men, rather than dreading proximity because of having the world's mind-set of helplessness in the presence of an attractive woman, need to surround themselves with simple accountability and sensible boundaries, while receiving counsel for any difficulties in their own marriages or personal lives.

For our part, we must forgive men (in general and in particular) for past wounds and repent of all judgments previously made against them, or we will defile those to whom we minister. We will reap what we sow. *If we are judgmental against men, we will not only encourage the disdain of men in other women, but prejudice against us will actually increase in the body.*

And if we think our value lies in our outward appearance, we must ask God to show us what He wants us to be *on the inside.* It's time to grow up!

With God's help and one another's prayers, we can all learn how to minister together in mutual respect. If we see ourselves and one another as Jesus does—as precious children for whom He gave His life—and realize that *He will avenge any evil we do to one another,* we will make sure we are held accountable to protect and cherish each other.

CAUSES AND PREVENTION

Now let's return to Sarah and Charles. What truly motivated

them? Was it love? Does love lead to sin?

Charles was coming on the scene full of discontentment and ungratefulness regarding his own marriage. He and his wife were having problems for which he was not taking responsibility. "If she would change..." "If she were like Sarah, then I would love her."

He also operated out of a vacuum—he had no one to hold him accountable for his thoughts and for how he spent his unsupervised time. He had no boundaries. *Bear in mind that his situation could be ours. What happens to men in leadership can happen to women in leadership just as easily.*

Sarah came on the scene lonely and unattached to anyone or any group that could have affirmed her. What should she have done to prevent the affair?

She should have:

1. Resisted having conversations with Charles in which they shared their hurts and personal problems.

2. Been in an accountable relationship with a mature Christian woman whom she trusted to be her sounding board for fluctuating emotions and to pray for her during trying times.

3. Been part of a small group that studied the Word together and took the time to have fun socially.

4. Gone home from work when everyone else did and refused to be alone with Charles behind closed doors.

6. Said *no* to compromising situations and fantasies even if he didn't, realizing that she is not a victim, but a child of God.

7. Checked her heart regularly to catch any desire to seduce, including not buying clothing designed to get a response from a man.

8. Bathed her life in prayer while practicing the presence of God, knowing He loved her and was with her every moment of the day and night.

9. Remembered that she is responsible to resist sin at all costs, but not responsible to solve Charles's problems.

BE FILLED WITH CHRIST

As more and more of us find ourselves serving in the ministry alongside men—whether in the pulpit, on the conference circuit, in counseling or business offices or on the mission field—maintaining sexual purity will be the greatest area of testing for most of us. Boundaries, accountability and counsel for past wounds *alone*—however wise to pursue—

won't bring safety, but these *plus* a grateful heart that cherishes intimacy with God above all else will keep us on track. We must remember that while we were created for intimacy, that need for intimacy must be filled by Christ, or our hunger and loneliness will draw, like a magnet, men to us who are unhealthy or uncommitted to purity of heart and mind.

As the gender wall slowly comes down, we must look within and raise our levels of personal integrity. *Pure, contented hearts are critically important, and we must determine to be held accountable to keep them that way.* There is no one, male or female, who can escape responsibility for protecting one another from sexual sin in the ministry and in the church.

TOGETHER

The site of the Symphony is being made ready. In God's design there will no longer be a male brass ensemble or a ladies' stringed quintet, but a grand extravaganza of beauty as we finally play together in safety, saving our hearts for Him! It will be music fit for a King!

"Maestro, the music please!"

Going Deeper

1. If you are single, what is wrong with sharing your personal heartaches with a married man when you are alone with him, or if you are married, with a man other than your husband?

2. Study Proverbs 5. Which verses can help protect you in your present situation?

3. Do you have any unconfessed sexual sin or spiritual adultery in your life? If so, make a plan now for repenting to God and confessing to a trusted spiritual advisor who can pray with you, pronounce you forgiven and separated from that person and hold you accountable to stay free.

4. What are the most effective ways for you to personally guard your heart and spirit from becoming knit illegally with a man?

5. How will you respond in the future to a man "of the cloth" who makes flirtatious or inappropriate advances toward you? What if you are attracted to him?

6. What are the warning signs that indicate a Christian man is looking to your love and affection to rescue him from his sorrows in life? How will you advise him?

Prayer of Commitment for Today:

_____

_____

_____

_____

_____

_____

_____

_____

_____

_____

The walk out to the end of the lane to the mailbox had never seemed so long! *Has it always been so great a distance?* Janet asked herself.

She was tired. The "knowing" was still in her heart, and the peace only a bit shaken, but she was indeed tired.

Reaching into the black mailbox that she had long ago decorated by painting bold yellow daisies on its sides, her hand touched more small white envelopes—notes of condolence she was sure. How hard everyone had taken Enoch's death! How comforting and loving they were to her!

Mixed in with the smaller envelopes was one very official-looking envelope with the return address of their church's denominational headquarters on it. Quickly opening it, she read:

Dear Mrs. Martin:

Please accept our deepest regrets over your husband's recent death. Everyone in the district had always held him in the highest esteem. We are praying daily for you and want you to contact us if we can be of service to you in any way.

We also wish to ask you to pray about a very serious matter. We have been receiving some unusual mail since his death. It seems that a great many people in your congregation want you to be their next pastor! They have expressed their admiration for your spiritual maturity and for the wisdom you have imparted to them over the years in many ways. They feel that you have long been a pastor to them, even if you didn't realize it, and now they want to make it official.

We at headquarters have reviewed the matter carefully and believe it to be in the best interest of the congregation and the denomination that you be appointed pastor of the Willow Heights Church.

Will you please pray about this and give it careful consideration? We will all be most honored to have you accept.

IN HIS SERVICE,
MATTHEW HENRY
DISTRICT SUPERINTENDENT

Can this be? she wondered, dazed. Janet read the letter again, then still again! And as if from a deep sleep the vision returned. Janet saw herself behind that simple pulpit, Bible open, text ready, her heart beating with joy! The faces came into focus before her eyes as they had so many times over the years, their expressions clearer than if they were standing with her right there by her mailbox!

Yes! Yes! The passion was still there, only it burned with a more disciplined flame than years ago.

As she turned and broke into a brisk walk back to the house, the "knowing" settled again into her spirit.

She would indeed be Willow Heights' first woman pastor.

12

✿

Forever in Tune

*But we have this treasure in jars of clay to show that
this all-surpassing power is from God and not from us.*
—2 CORINTHIANS 4:7

We may be *amazed* at what God will lead us to do in the
years ahead—the intimidating places in which we may
find ourselves and the "mighty" men we may be asked to
address. Feelings of inadequacy may threaten to paralyze us—
or they may open the way to a much deeper understanding
of God's power and anointing.

A FRESH REVELATION

One gentle spring evening, in a somewhat reflective and melancholy mood, I drove alone to a quiet retreat center in Virginia Beach. I wandered into the cafe and purchased a cup of coffee, then carried it out into the reception area, looking for just the right spot to relax and think. It was a slow, easy, quiet Sunday night at the inn with people drifting here and there, chatting in little groups. Occasionally some clever remark sparked light laughter among them.

Two men were alternating at the grand piano in the hall, playing whatever they enjoyed most and taking requests from passersby. I settled in on one of the Victorian couches across the room from them and listened as I sipped my coffee.

They played well, and the music slowly seeped into my weary soul. I ruefully mused, however, that it seems that I have never been outstanding at anything I have ever done: jack of all trades, master of none. Whether it was music, sports, academics, writing, teaching... there were always many others who were much better at it than I.

The men finished playing, gathered their jackets and soda cans and strolled by me on their way out. One stopped by my couch and curiously remarked to me, "You play too, don't you?"

Startled by his insight and candor, I replied, "Oh, but not nearly as well as you do!" I had hardly touched a piano in two years. The few times I had played had been only the songs I

166

had written several years ago during the searing Refiner's fire experience. They were simple melodies, and I was an unaccomplished, common musician. I had long ago come to accept my position on the "couch of life" musically.

"Go ahead and play something," he grinned as he motioned toward the beautiful ebony instrument standing majestically alone in the great room.

I just smiled in return and shook my head.

They left. In fact, everyone else left and the room was empty. If there had been even one person remaining, I would not have moved.

Surprising myself, I arose and went to the piano, adjusted the seat and slowly placed my hands on the smooth ivory keys. I began to hear the music in my heart, and my fingers hesitatingly responded to the melody.

The sound flowing from that instrument was incredible! The vaulted ceiling and deep carpeting softened yet caught the vibrancy of the strings and sent the music aloft in absolute beauty!

I grew bold and pressed in. As my heart poured itself out in simplicity upon the keys, the music intensified under my fingertips. I found myself weaving melodies rich in nuances I had never been able to produce before!

I had the strongest impression that the Father Himself was showing me how, that He was teaching me and strengthening my timid heart! It slowly dawned upon me that this very music must have been in His imagination long before He gave it to me. I was surely not the creator!

Before I knew it there was a young lady watching over my shoulder. "That's beautiful!" she murmured. Suddenly I was aware that several people had filtered into the reception area and were listening.

When the song ended, someone applauded and called out, "More! More!"

Rather than making me nervous, the attention brought on a calmness that was new to me. I continued playing until I knew that I had learned what the Father had drawn me there that evening to learn.

The light of my understanding came on! You see, *He* wrote the music, not I! And best of all, He can reproduce His artistry through me and make even my simplest gift touch hearts and cause them to praise Him!

GOD'S DESIRE

That experience did not mean that I was meant to be a concert pianist! It symbolized something much more significant.

It spoke deeply to me about God's creative power within each of His children—even me. It reaffirmed His interest in my life, His desire and plan to make my life a song that would bless others and cause me to walk even more closely with Him.

It told me that I was loved and that the least I had to offer Him would surely be enough, for it would be by *His* power that lives would be changed if I were obedient to Him. After all, the passion in my heart was born in His heart first.

THE ANOINTING

That experience demonstrated the essence of God's anointing process: *His* life-changing power is released through inadequate instruments willing to share His simple truth, instruments trusting His hand upon them more than the stuff of which they are made.

We are not to judge ourselves against others, but only to do our best with pure hearts, using whatever measure of ability He has given us, trusting Him to give it His beauty.

That we have little talent can be a benefit for us. When God blesses what we do, we too will see Jesus, as surely as will those who watch and listen, for we will know that it was not we but He who brought the power.

If we constantly evaluate our abilities against the talents and successes of others, we will never move beyond the weakest forms of ministry. It will be as though we are choking the Holy Spirit with our bare hands! We will lose the vision of *His* glory and *His* perfection, and no one will see Jesus and be set free.

NOTHING TO FEAR

We have nothing to fear but fear itself—and that has been overcome by His perfect love. He will never lead us where He will not direct us and give us the words to say and the wisdom to act in honor to His name.

And wherever we go, our integrity will be our protection

as long as we remain teachable, small in our own eyes, accountable and willing to obey no matter what the cost. If our lives are an act of worship to the living God, whatever man might say in criticism of us will be dealt with by the Almighty Himself! We need not waste our energy trying to defend our obedience.

But if we sin—if we begin to worship ourselves and think that we own the music, unwilling to share our authority or release it altogether if God sees fit to put us upon the shelf for a season—there is good news! We will be able to find Him again at a single cry. He is quick to forgive a heart that is broken and contrite over sin, and restoration is at the core of all He does.

DISCIPLINE

When discipline comes for our wrongdoing, we can take great comfort in knowing that we are in the hands of God—not man. However, God may use an unbroken vessel to mete it out. Discipline is part of His loving plan. We will see the purpose clearly in the end. There must be no protest, only gratitude that our wretched flesh is being stricken.

When we love Him with undivided hearts, nothing will be able to keep us from being a glory unto Him. He will see that our deepest desires—the passion in our spirits for His presence and His purpose—will be granted. The music will pour from our lives—a praise to the God who has called us by name.

IF WE LOSE OUR WAY

Through the seasons of obscurity or in the fires of adversity and service we may lose the passion that had once burned white hot. The vision may lose its shape, drifting quickly out of focus like the shifting clouds on a windy day. At those times it may seem that our very lives are ebbing away and that we are helpless to stop the gray shades of death from overtaking us. During those dreadful days we are to ask God what part our own will may have played in bringing the darkness.

When, in the fray of battle, did we take offense and let it turn to bitterness? Did we sin against another and not repent? Had we become undisciplined or selfish? Had we taken on more than He had asked us to in order to please others or impress them? Were we spending sufficient time with the Father daily and practicing His presence constantly? Had we become cocky and independent, unwilling to make difficult changes in our lives?

Again, forgiveness is just a cry away. We will learn, slowly but surely, to study our hearts and know our own patterns of weakness so that we can be ever on the alert for the dangers. We will learn to walk securely, playing our instruments in holiness and joy.

REFRESHED

In solitude we will hear His song in the breezes that stir the pages of our lives and show us chapters that are yet to come. As we spend time with other visionaries and passionate lovers of God and allow ourselves to dream again, the flame will be rekindled. He will fill our hearts with fresh spiritual oil, speak *rhema* from His Word and send us unsought encouragement from those who walk with God.

The wind will stop blowing and the clouds stay put. And as our eyes search the skies, the vision will reappear, cast clearly in the heavens. This time we will leave it in the hands of the Father without grasping or playing God.

And as we embrace the vision and feel the passion burn again, the music will return. But it will not be the strident melody that boasts of our personal power, nor will it be the tenuous tone that quivers with fear. Instead, the strings and the brass and the finely tooled woodwinds in our hands will be forever in tune with the Father's voice and resonate with holy power.

And the Glory will come.

Going Deeper

1. Describe a time when you felt that God gave you a supernatural grace to do something that you thought was beyond your ability. What understanding of God's faithfulness did you learn from that experience?

2. How do you define *the anointing?*

3. What does Proverbs 27:21 mean to you ("The crucible for silver and the furnace for gold, but man is tested by the praise he receives")?

4. What is your plan in the event you must be disciplined for wrongdoing in the ministry? Based on the Word of God, how have you determined you will respond to correction?

5. What is your plan, based on the Word of God, for addressing sin in someone *under* your authority? What will you do if the sin is in someone *over* you in authority?

6. Name five things or conditions in your life that could destroy the passion that fuels your vision for ministry.

7. Name or describe five things or activities that God can use to restore your passion and your will to go on in spite of difficulties.

Prayer of Commitment for Today:

A Prayer

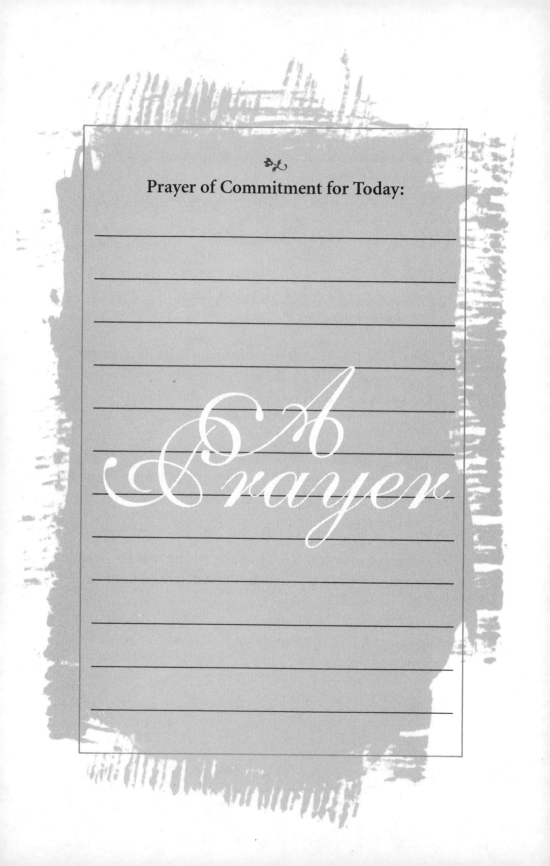

13

❦

In the Maestro's Presence

You have made known to me the path of life; you will fill me with joy in your presence, with eternal pleasures at your right hand.

—PSALM 16:11

If there is one thing of which we must be sure, it is that God loves us. This is accepted at first by an act of faith, and then it is learned deeply in His presence.

JOY IN BEING TOGETHER

A friend of mine recently told me the story of his first backpacking trip with his three-year-old daughter. All day it seemed that he was saying, "Don't touch that; it's poisonous!" or "Don't put your hand into that groundhog hole!" Twice he had to pick Missy up and remove ticks from her skin, which made the little tyke cry. But at the end of the day as this young father drove home, his little girl asleep with her curly head on his shoulder, he knew that they had had a *wonderful* time—because they had been together. So it is with God and us.

God loves being with us, even if we sometimes do dumb things and have to be corrected or redirected. He enjoys being with us because He loves us—no matter what. He longs for our company every day.

THE TREASURE

God doesn't demand our presence; He waits for us to give ourselves to Him freely. The gift we give of our attentiveness is an incomparable treasure! Lazarus's sister Mary gave that gift to the Lord one day long ago. Listen to what Mary might have told us if we had been with her that day:

> It seemed an odd time to do nothing. Jesus and all twelve of His disciples dropped in on us unexpectedly, and just at mealtime! Martha sprang into action to fix dinner and serve the men, and normally I would have done the same.
>
> But something unexplainable grabbed at my heart and made me unable to leave His side. I couldn't take

my eyes off His face! All I wanted to do was study every change of expression, memorize the nuances in His voice and cling to His presence as though I might never see Him again!

Martha was, of course, furious, and I sensed the disciples were annoyed as well. After all, women were supposed to serve the men and then stay out of sight— not relax with them in the living room! But in that moment, I didn't care what they thought. To be with Jesus meant more to me than the dictates of custom or the demands of the moment.

As I sank to the floor at His feet, He shifted slightly on His couch to give me a comfortable place there, His face breaking into a smile. The disciples, forever trying to adjust to Jesus' unpredictable behavior, felt awkward but said nothing. I kept my eyes fixed on Him. He alone could send me away... and He didn't!

As He talked of kingdom matters—of life and death and the heart of His Father—I listened, taking in every mood of His heart. It seemed important that I, just as much as the disciples, grasp His mission and understand His love. There was a long journey ahead, and we all needed to know that He would give us direction and strength.

In His presence, no matter what might lie head, I was at peace. Soldiers could have broken down the door and put us in chains and I wouldn't have been afraid!

He loves me! I know that now because I experienced it during those precious hours at His feet. As I gave Him the gift of my heart, in return He filled every empty space in my life with His love.

Best of all, He was very pleased that I had stayed! He even told Martha that He wished she had left the work behind and done the same! I feel sorry now for her that she missed all that I enjoyed.

That day, food wasn't on His mind; that day only our relationship was worth spending time on. That I chose Him over labor blessed us both so much. All He had wanted was my heart!

TODAY

And so it is with us today. All He wants is our hearts. Service follows when the time is right, but sensitivity to what is *best*, and *when*, are important lessons to learn.

It is in His presence, when we give Him our hearts, that we remember our reason for living and the worth of it all. It is in His presence that we are healed in mind, will and emotions time and time again. It is as we worship Him deeply that He ministers to us, that He holds us close and clears our vision so that we see the victory close at hand, even when we've nearly lost hope. It is as we press into the holy of holies that His purposes are revealed. It's there that we fall in love with Him all over again!

Jesus Himself was an example to us. When great crowds

awaited Him or clamored for His touch and attention, He often turned the other way and sought the Father in a lonely place instead. Intimacy with the One who loved and understood Him better than anyone meant more to Him than even doing "good" things. That pattern is, unfortunately, so unlike the one that we so easily follow today. We usually run to the crowds and the needs, neglecting His presence!

THE TRUTH

People who bear His name must know the way into His presence well and travel it daily, forgetting life's demands and the expectations of others, content to sit at His feet. This is critical—not optional. If we can't find His love, if we're at a loss as to how to give Him our own in worship, we are in deep trouble. Nothing we will ever try to give in ministry can rival in importance or significance the ability to find His presence.

Christians who forget how to find Him in personal worship—who are too busy performing—will never bear fruit that remains. Those who speak His name but abide only in the land of urgent service will fall into despair long before a single godly goal is reached.

We cannot live without Him, without being able to grab hold of His love, without knowing how to tuck ourselves away in the secret place at a moment's notice. We cannot endure to the end without living by the strength of His life freely reigning within us.

We are *nothing* without Him. Granted, with Him we are

like grass and the flower that fades, but we are breathing holy breath and given eternal life—unconditional gifts from God! How wonderful!

But without experiencing the love that awaits us in His presence we suffer immeasurable torture. To know Him from a distance is harder than if we'd never met Him at all! We know what we're missing, and it will eventually break our hearts.

So what does He want from us? Those very hearts. However, they can't be given at a distance.

INTIMACY THWARTED

Sometimes it is hard to tell which comes first for some of us— our not believing that He loves us and therefore being unable to find intimacy with Him, or our being unable to find intimacy with Him and therefore not believing that He loves us.

If we have never experienced unconditional love, if no one has ever delighted in our sheer presence, we will have to deal with this fundamental issue before we do anything else. We cannot minister His life to others without knowing beyond a shadow of a doubt that He loves us "no matter what."

INTIMACY FOUND

A great healing will come if we will separate those who didn't know how to love us from our view of God by forgiving them. Through forgiveness we will be released from our expectation that God will visit us with the same pain we have experienced at the hands of human fathers and authority figures. God is like none other! He will melt our stony hearts if we will drop the barriers we erected when hurt before.

Then we must learn all we can about the One who gave His life for us. As we ask Him, the Holy Spirit will reveal deep truths to us about His love and faithfulness.

Even though we may have been believers for many years, we may need to choose to trust Him now. Our faith will begin its marvelous journey from our minds to our hearts, and we will fall in love with Him in return.

And then we can imagine sitting at His feet as Mary did. As we savor His presence, we will learn a deeper song than that of human zeal. As we close ourselves away in deep worship and quiet, waiting for Him to speak, He will.

SPENDING TIME WITH HIM

Embracing His presence in solitude, as well as in the midst of other believers, is indispensable. Whether we find it walking along a wooded path, sitting alone in our favorite hideaway with the Word open on our laps or in the congregation, He will be there with us. As we give Him our hearts, we will feel His love.

In whatever place, in whatever way by which we fix our eyes on Him, He will return the gaze. He waits for us and calls us by name. The choice to pursue Him is ours, as it was Mary's. No service surpasses this or has life without it.

To be one with Him in a divine exchange of love will ensure that the music that flows from our lives will remain sweet and pure. There is indeed no other way it can be done. Christ *in* us continues to be our only hope of glory.

LIFESTYLE OF INTIMACY

The strength of our lives and of any ministry organization or effort we establish will rise or fall on our willingness to withdraw from the press and be alone with Him, lifting His name on high. It is in His presence—when He has our undivided attention—that the richest songs are born and God's love instilled in our hearts.

In the Maestro's presence, His love finds our hearts and changes us. In His presence, strength and wisdom are discovered. And in His presence, we find joy for the journey.

GOING DEEPER

1. What is your perception of God's love when He convicts you personally of sin? Do you really believe that God loves you unconditionally?

2. How free are you in giving Him your love and adoration? Is there something standing in the way of loving Him with abandonment?

3. Do you feel more comfortable working for Him or spending time with Him? Have you found a balance?

4. When do you most clearly feel His affirmation of you and sense His direction for your life?

5. What is really the point of ministering to others?

6. Do you have a place of solitude, a place where you can simply be with Him and listen for Him without having to *do* anything or *say* anything "spiritual"?

7. Besides practicing His presence in solitude, are you faithfully absorbing the Word of God, interceding for others, actively learning from teachers of the Word?

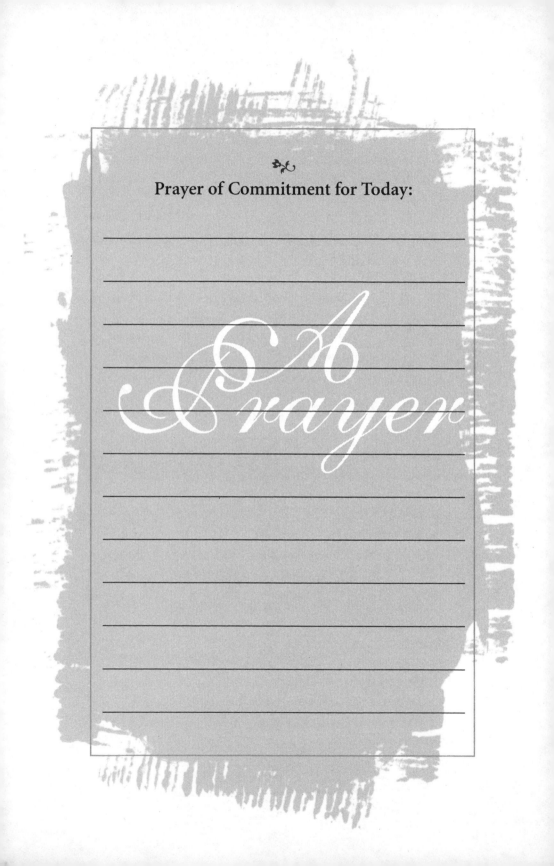

Prayer of Commitment for Today:

Prayer

Conclusion

May God himself, the God of peace, sanctify you through and through. May your whole spirit, soul and body be kept blameless at the coming of our Lord Jesus Christ. The one who calls you is faithful and he will do it.

—1 THESSALONIANS 5:23–24

The Symphony is assembling, instrument by precious instrument, across America and around the world. Women everywhere are listening for His voice and obeying His call. As we yield the control of every part of our lives to Him, we find ourselves fully qualified to play for the King of kings.

CAUTIONS

When we seek to be obedient in ministry we learn many things—some of them the hard way by making mistakes and suffering for them. We find that remaining teachable is our greatest asset!

After reflecting on my own times of uncertainty, fear and ineptitude, I have developed a list of cautions that would have helped me greatly had someone passed them on to me when I needed them. Now I give them to you with the prayer that each of you will take them seriously, writing those most relevant to you on your bathroom mirror if necessary!

1. Do not make decisions based upon someone's "prophetic word" to you.

When one is given, store it away and then continue pursuing intimacy with God and faithfulness to that which is at hand in your life. If it is a true word, God will speak it to you personally as well. Even then, wait for His direction and timing in bringing it to pass. (Usually He fulfills it after you have forgotten it!) Others' words should be confirming, not directing. A wise prophet is as careful about *when* to release the word as *what* the word says and will not give it as instruction. Too many naïve believers charge ahead to make words come true long before they have heard from God or have been prepared for the work.

2. When you are a guest speaker in someone else's church, find out what your hosts prefer in dress, and then choose your clothing accordingly.

Honor their traditions, or your liberty will be a stumbling block to their hearing your message.

3. If you are leading a retreat and want to conclude with communion, find out first if the sponsoring church or organization allows women to serve the elements.

Some denominations adamantly support only the pastor or elders serving communion and will be outraged if you attempt it. Such a misstep can spoil an otherwise wonderful retreat. It is not a matter of right or wrong, but one of respect for your host church. Do not make it a matter of discussion. You are simply a guest.

4. Don't put on an "anointed" voice when you ascend the platform to speak.

Be yourself. Honesty and transparency will always carry the day. After I had taught several sessions at a ministry training institute in Florida, a man from the class approached me to tell me that he had been able to receive instruction from me because I didn't try to sound like a man and because I was the same person on and off the platform. My honesty had broken down his prejudice against women and helped him absorb what I had to say out of the Word of God.

You see, the anointing comes because of God's presence operating within our obedience. Trying to sound or look like someone who is more forceful does nothing to increase our authority—in fact, it can destroy the anointing because such behavior is dishonest and motivated by the fear of man.

5. Remember always the sin of which you are capable if left to yourself.

Stay accountable to someone wiser than you, someone unafraid to tell you the truth, someone with whom you have covenanted to receive words of correction and encouragement.

6. If you sin in any way that affects the people to whom or with whom you minister, confess it to them and ask their forgiveness.

If you hide it out of embarrassment or fear, whatever was within you that caused the sin will continue to grow. Eventually it will destroy you and damage untold others. Give people an opportunity to practice forgiveness, and then embrace whatever discipline your authorities deem appropriate. If they overreact, don't fight it. You are not in the hands of man, but in the hands of God!

7. Hold ministry lightly and in open hands.

Continually remember that it came from God, and He can choose to end this "season" of ministry whenever He desires. Never take ownership of it, or it will viciously take ownership of you and you will miss the voice of God.

8. Spend more time nurturing your family than pursuing your ministry.

If you run ahead of God and minister outside the home while there is still opposition and anger in your family over it, you will find yourself easily deceived and easy prey for spiritual adultery or sexual sin in the ministry workplace.

9. Get inner healing counseling for wounds and sins in your own past.

Do not allow Satan to have grounds by which to claim entrance into your life and ministry.

10. Remember that any bitterness harbored in your heart will be sown alongside the Word that you speak.

You will minister out of a defiled spirit, and the people will become defiled.

11. Seek affiliation with a body with whom you can worship and from whom you are willing to learn.

Be sure that you are open and honest with them at all times, and report regularly to them.

12. Ask God to give you committed intercessors.

Whenever possible, take one with you when you speak or minister.

13. Don't travel long distances alone.

Billy Graham has made traveling with others a career policy, and it has protected him from scandal many times. It is wisdom.

14. Don't minister out of what others expect of you.

Seek God for your place, message and method. Remain open to change.

15. Don't ever think that you are too busy or too indispensable to take vacations and sabbaticals.

Being spiritually refreshed will restore your perspective and renew creativity. Also, others need to learn to serve you by standing in the gap for you while you are away.

16. Don't kick open doors to minister.

Learn to wait for God to prepare the way. In the waiting you will learn to die to self and trust Him. This lesson is essential to any effectiveness in the ministry.

17. Become invisible to yourself.

Then others will see only Jesus, and lives will be changed.

JOY IN THE JOURNEY

It may not be an easy journey, but there will be joy! Whenever the Song of the Redeemed rises in simple majesty from willing hearts, there is a celebration in heaven! And when we are asked *why* we are willing to give our lives to play the King's melodies, sometimes in the face of ridicule, we can answer with confidence as Eric Liddel did in the movie *Chariots of Fire.* When his sister asked the Olympic runner why he must run, he responded with passion, "Because God made me fast. And when I run, I feel His pleasure!"[1] God has created us to be instruments for His glory in ways unique to us according to our giftings. And when we play His music, we too will feel His pleasure!

He will love us through everything as He teaches us to be honest and straightforward, compassionate to the wounded and needy and to suffer injustice with sweet dignity. Wherever there is the most pain, we will surely see His footprints just ahead of us, for He has walked that way before.

Most of all, He will be faithful. He will never leave us nor forsake us (Heb. 13:5). This He promised, and He is a keeper of His Word!

So let the Song rise! Let the music flow in power and grace from these lives that have become at last...

Instruments for His Glory!

Notes

❦

CHAPTER 1
AN IRRESISTIBLE SONG

1. L. E. Maxwell, *Women in Ministry* (Camp Hill, PA: Christian Publications, 1987), 108.

2. Ibid., 109

3. Ibid., 110.

4. Ibid., 111.

5. Herbert Kane, *Life and Work on the Mission Field* (Grand Rapids, MI: Baker Book House, 1980), 143.

CHAPTER 7
GIVING UP FIRST CHAIR IN THE SYMPHONY

1. Joyce Strong, *Lambs on the Ledge* (Camp Hill, PA: Christian Publishing, 1995), 149–151. Used by permission.

CONCLUSION

1. Warner Bros., Inc., *Chariots of Fire* (Burbank, CA: Time Warner Co., 1981).

Recommended Reading

Bilezikian, Gilbert. *Beyond Sex Roles: What the Bible Says About a Woman's Place in Church and Family.* Grand Rapids, MI: Baker Books, 1985.

Clinton, Dr. J. Robert. *The Making of a Leader.* Colorado Springs, CO: NavPress, 1988.

Grenz, Stanley J. *Women in the Church: A Biblical Theology of Women in Ministry.* Westmont, IL: InterVarsity Press, 1995.

Groothuis, Rebecca Merrill. *Women Caught in the Conflict: The Culture War Between Traditionalism and Feminism.* Grand Rapids, MI: Baker Books, 1994.

Lutz, Lorry and Christenson, Evelyn. *Women As Risk-Takers for God.* Grand Rapids, MI: Baker Book House, 1997.

Malcolm, Kari Torjesen. *Women at the Crossroads.* Westmont, IL: InterVarsity Press, 1982.

Strong, Joyce. *Lambs on the Ledge: Seeing and Avoiding Dangers in Doing God's Work.* Camp Hill, PA: Christian Publications, Inc., 1995.

——.*Caught in the Crossfire.* Camp Hill, PA: Christian Publications, Inc., 1999.

Publications Available on
Gifts Identification

ॐ

Decker, John. *Releasing Spiritual Gifts*. P.O. Box 3631, Bend, OR 97707-0631. (541) 593-7774, (541) 593-7479 (fax).

DeVries, Thomas K. *Discovering Our Gifts*. New York: Paulist Press, 1986.

Harbaugh, Gary L. *God's Gifted People: Discovering and Using Your Spiritual and Personal Gifts*. Minneapolis, MN: Augsburg Fortress Press, 1988.

Myers-Briggs Type Indicator. Consulting Psychologists Press, Inc., 3803 E. Bayshore Rd., Palo Alto, CA 94303. (800) 624-1765, 1988.

O'Conner, Elizabeth. *Eighth Day of Creation: Discovering Your Gifts and Using Them*. Waco, TX: Word Books, 1971.

Packo, John E. *Find and Use Your Spiritual Gifts*. Camp Hill, PA: Christian Publications, Inc.

Helpful Organizations
Regarding Spiritual Gifts

AIM
Cedar Park, Texas
(512) 331-8263

Birkman Method
Houston, Texas
(713) 623-2760

Breakthru
LEAD Consulting
Raleigh, North Carolina
(919) 783-0354

Discovery Ministry
Frisco, Texas
(972) 335-8150

Mobilizing Spiritual Gifts
Albuquerque, New Mexico
(505) 296-8568

The Profile Leadership Institute
Aurora, Colorado
(303) 745-2097 (fax)

To contact the author to speak at your church, conference or retreat, please send your request in writing to:

Joyce Strong
P.O. Box 58452
Raleigh, NC 27658

You can experience more of God's grace & *love!*

If you would like free information on how you can know God more deeply and experience His grace, love and power more fully in your life, simply write or e-mail us. We'll be delighted to send you information that will be a blessing to you.

To check out other titles from **Creation House** that will impact your life, be sure to visit your local Christian bookstore, or call this toll-free number:

1-800-599-5750

For free information from Creation House:

CREATION HOUSE
600 Rinehart Rd.
Lake Mary, FL 32746
www.creationhouse.com